SECRET BARROW-IN-FURNESS

Gill Jepson

AMBERLEY

About the Author

Gill Jepson is an author of children's novels and local history books. She has a teaching background and a passionate love of history, particularly that of the Furness Peninsula and Furness Abbey. She is chair of Furness Abbey Fellowship, which works in partnership with English Heritage to assist the extension of the heritage of Furness Abbey. *Secret Barrow-in-Furness* is her second publication for Amberley, the previous being *Barrow-in-Furness Through Time*. She delivers talks on local history and writes regular articles for the online magazine *Huddlehub*. She is a Patron of Reading and regularly visits schools. Details of her other books can be found on www.out-of-time.co.uk

First published 2017

Amberley Publishing
The Hill, Stroud
Gloucestershire, GL5 4EP

www.amberley-books.com

ISBN 978 1 4456 6846 8 (print)
ISBN 978 1 4456 6847 5 (ebook)

British Library Cataloguing in Publication Data.
A catalogue record for this book is available from the British Library.

Origination by Amberley Publishing.
Printed in Great Britain.

Contents

Introduction

Secret Barrow-in-Furness is concerned with those less obvious places that hide interesting historical facts and evidence. In some sense it is history that is hidden rather than 'secrets', but over time these locations become forgotten and when rediscovered are important clues to the past. This book attempts to highlight these lesser-known places and discover something of their background history. Some of the evidence is scant and one wonders how much will be remembered within a couple of generations. My hope is that I can record some of these and capture those places that could very easily be swept away with new development and building. Some of the locations are already at risk and without a written and photographic record can very quickly be consigned to memory only. Local people will recognise many of the items catalogued in this book, but I hope to add some depth and dimension to the bare facts.

I will be including Barrow's powerful Victorian legacy, which is more obvious, but it would be remiss of me not to investigate the earlier history too. This peninsula has a signature and unique response to the historical record and far from being a 'cul-de-sac', as proclaimed by many commentators, it has played a key part in national history, sometimes briefly, but nevertheless significantly. One example of this is the landing on Piel of Lambert Simnel the pretender; yet how many people when picnicking there in the summer realise such an event occurred.

My intention for this book is to demonstrate that Barrow is not perhaps what it first seems. It has a certain reputation as a post-industrial town, yet has one of the most successful shipbuilding companies as its main employer – recently acquiring more contracts for national defence projects. It has a worldwide reputation, whether retrospectively for the steel industry – now defunct – or currently for its nuclear submarine production. Barrow like many places has social issues and areas of deprivation, and these recently attracted attention because another author, J. K. Rowling – under her Robert Galbraith pseudonym – wrote about the town. The description is not always attractive or wholly representative, but we have to claim this as our own just as much as the leafier and more beautiful aspects, like Furness Abbey. Every effort has been made to provide a full and comprehensive record of historical facts to accompany the photographs.

I have been generous in my assessment of what constitutes Barrow-in-Furness. This is so that outlying settlements that were previously more significant than Barrow can be included. The Furness Peninsula is unique geographically and all the settlements are parts of a greater whole. It would be unacceptable to only focus on the town of Barrow.

Hopefully, this book will ameliorate the negative image Barrow sometimes suffers from and demonstrate that it has many facets and is a jewel in the Furness crown. I hope that the reader will view Barrow-in-Furness in a different light and discover the hidden layers of history over many centuries. It allows an investigation of the best that is Barrow and demonstrates that there is much to love about it, if one takes the time to look.

1. A Northern Powerhouse

Barrow-in-Furness is in many ways unique. Until 1845 it was a small village of 200 people, quiet and fairly unremarkable. Within forty years its population jumped to more than 50,000. The town had grown because of the railway and industry, which opened up the area and drew in hundreds of workers from places like Dudley, Cornwall, Scotland and Ireland. This produced a melting pot of people, overwhelming the small indigenous population and creating a strange linguistic mix emerging as a 'Barra' accent. The town fathers initiated building programmes that would be the envy of developers today. The small triangle in which the original village sat was from the Town Hall to St George's Church and Dalton Road. Dalton Road, the oldest road, ran north-east towards what is now Abbey Road. This small embryonic Barrow presents the only organic road system: the remainder is planned and designed as a rectilinear grid. The wide roads and well-designed housing were a showcase for the town council, proclaiming the modernity and civic pride that was already evident. The building process was essential if the increased population was going to be housed in sanitary and comfortable circumstances. The initial influx proved a headache for James Ramsden (later the first mayor) and he remarked that if he built a thousand homes, the following week he would need a thousand more. Early housing had been makeshift, temporary, overcrowded and unsanitary.

Overcrowding was a major factor in planning the town. Disease and epidemic was a huge driver for the council and the inappropriate accommodation such as the huts on Barrow Island, hastily built to accommodate workers, was swept away in preference for tenements and rows of terraced houses. These were an immense improvement and when first built they were classed as model and modern housing. The Victorian paternalism prevailed and housing was placed as close to the workplace as possible. This was not necessarily for the convenience of the workforce, but ensured that they were never far from the workplace. Additionally, housing provided by the employer had a two-fold purpose. Decent housing closely attached to the job was an incentive for the worker, while at the same time ensuring that a proportion of the wages returned to the employer in rent. This system was a very astute method of tying the worker to the job and offsetting costs for the employer. In short, it was not dissimilar to the feudal system of tied accommodation. The flats have been refurbished and brought up to modern standards – for example the Devonshire Buildings, still administered by Holker Estates (the Cavendish family), which are now attractive modern apartments with the facilities we expect today.

Little evidence remains of the original buildings in Barrow village. The whole village was home to around 200 people. It was rural and before the advent of the Furness Railway there were piers on the channel between Barrow Island and Barrow village; from here slate and iron ore was loaded. There are some good sources to refer to from this time, including William Fisher's Diary. He was a local farmer and left behind him a snapshot of the village at the time. The original confines of the village followed the line along Dalton Lane (Dalton Road) – one of the few early roads into the area – to Rabbit Hill (St George's Hill) and back to the Town Hall. This small triangle became the heart of the new town. The first railway station and offices were located at Rabbit Hill and the town grew and took in the area along the water's edge, now called The Strand. W. B. Kendall's map of 1843 shows the size and location of the original village; this area is now absorbed into a larger townscape and is hardly identifiable as Barrowhead as it was sometimes known. One wall close to Schneider Square is probably one of the farm walls from the early settlement, another can be found near Rabbit Hill at the entrance to Cavendish Docks. The centre of the town shifted over time and this end of town is now at the edge. However, there are plans to develop this area significantly, creating new housing in a marina development, which will certainly be a new departure if it comes to fruition.

DID YOU KNOW?

Barrow Borough Council has a Satsuma bowl given to the town at the launch of the *Mikasa* battleship, built at Vickers Shipyard in Barrow. The bowl and an original copy of the menu from the launch (in English and Japanese) on 8 January 1900 are kept in the Town Hall in commemoration of the event. A street in Walney also bears the ship's name.

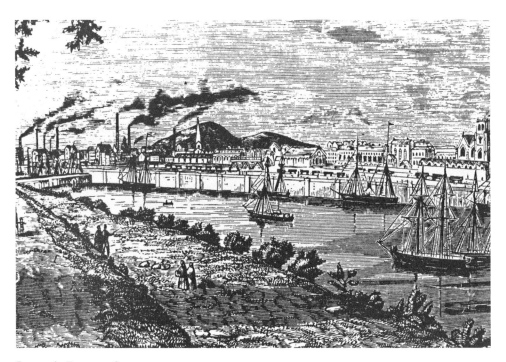

Barrow-in-Furness, 1870.

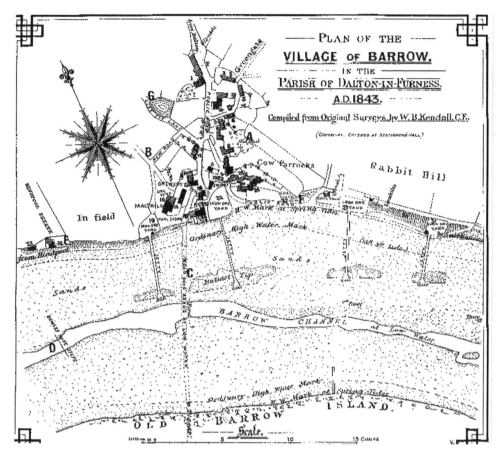

Barrow Village, W. B. Kendall, from a tithe map of 1842 (BNFC).

Furness Railway

The Furness Railway began as a line along the coast to transport slate and iron ore to the embryonic port of Barrow. This replaced the horse-drawn carts and pack horses used in the early days of the industry, the slate and iron ore being shipped to various points on the Furness coast. The town developed around the railway, but it eventually pushed into the outskirts and branched off in various directions to enable the workforce to reach the mines and to connect the area further afield. William Fisher in his diary remarks in 1841 that 'the Harbour Master entered up his situation at Barrow also same Day the Wet (Thwaite) Flat Iron Ore was first led to Barrow'. Little did he realise that this would have far-reaching changes for his town but also his own farm and way of life.

John Abel Smith, who bought Roa Island in 1840, changed the island forever. He built a causeway across from the mainland at Rampside and a deepwater pier to allow steamers to dock from Fleetwood. In 1846 William Fisher in his diary mentions that the railway line from Roa Island to Dalton opened for passengers. It is interesting to note that Roa Island and Rampside were regarded as a bathing resort in the late eighteenth and early nineteenth centuries

A goods line was extended to Roa, attaching the Furness Railway line from Kirkby. Soon a passenger service began but there was a dispute over the use of the pier. In 1852 the railway agreed to buy the lease for the island but before the deal was struck a storm destroyed the pier. This allowed the railway company to buy the island estate cheaply and continue the service until 1891. The pier was demolished due to the silting up of the channel but the railway continued until 1936. The causeway is now a road, but looking carefully one can find evidence of the stone sleepers along the sides.

The station, which was at the end of the causeway, is no longer apparent but the hostelry built in 1849 as the Piel Pier Hotel is still there. It is an attractive building and it changed its name in 1890 to the Roa Island Hotel. It was a popular pub and eating place but it has now become a private home.

The railway and the iron ore mines would have been hazardous and hard work, and William Fisher catalogues a list of disasters and accidents, which highlight the serious and dangerous nature of work in the early years of industrial development. In 1828 he reports that two miners were 'sufacated by the foul air at Crosgates Iron Ore pit', again in 1838 two men suffocated at Stainton mine when the pit head caught fire and smoke and fumes descended to the pit below and killed them. Of course there were many roof falls and subsidence reported, with loss of life and even drowning because of flooding in Park Mine pit due to a pond bursting. These are little-known facts, which many observers of the environmental evidence of the mines today are unaware of.

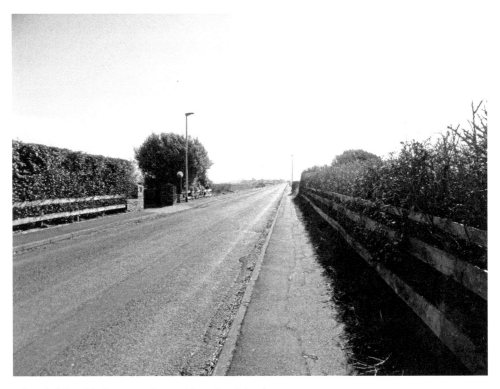

John Abel Smith's Causeway Rampside to Roa Island.

The railway was no better. Accidents reported frequently in Fisher's diary seem horrific and careless today, but we are dealing with a time when such machinery was new and unfamiliar. In 1846 he mentions poor William Wilson, a twenty-two-year-old labourer who 'through inadvertence' was caught between two moving wagons and shattered his knee. Sadly seven days later he died, probably due to infection – we tend to forget that broken limbs in the past could be fatal. Again in 1847 a man called Spencer was apparently killed by three railway wagons running over him, breaking his thighs – he survived for two hours after the accident and one can only hope he was unconscious.

Fisher makes reference to James Ramsden in his diary, which is indicative of his increasing importance in the town; it sits among other announcements and records of the mundane, like sowing oats in 1853. Ramsden was making his mark by now and would be known across the district and obviously Fisher regarded it important enough to note down Ramsden's marriage. The tone of the insertion is formal and one can assume he took it from the newspaper report. The marriage between James Ramsden and Annie Mary Edwards took place in June 1853 in Wallasey, and Revd W. Pollock officiated. Later in 1859 we see that Mrs Ramsden had delivered a son at 'Abbots House'.

Tacked onto this entry is one which was more significant than he could have imagined. He remarks that the Iron Furnaces were opened at Hindpool, Barrow. This event was 'witnessed by several gentlemen who came by special Train on the 18th October owners Messrs Hannah (Hannay) and Schneider, it was a Galla and a beautiful day for the season.' So began the complete industrialisation of Barrow.

2. Iron and Steel: The Red Earth

Barrow-in-Furness in its heyday was an important iron producer and steel manufacturer and it is said that steel rails made in Barrow were of the highest quality and could be found from Canada to South Africa. One of the reasons that Barrow grew during the Industrial Revolution was due to the discovery of the extremely rich iron ore deposit at the Park mine near Askam. H. W. Schneider began to export the ore to Wales and Staffordshire but as soon as the railway connection was completed the possibilities to expand the town became apparent. In 1857 with Robert Hannay, a Scottish iron industrialist, Schneider built three blast furnaces to enable the processing of the ore locally, thus increasing efficiency and profit. Limestone was available locally and coke could be shipped in from Durham. In 1856 Henry Bessemer invented a better and cheaper method of processing iron ore; luckily the type of ore found in Furness was suitable for this process.

James Ramsden formed a steel company in 1864, because he could see the advantage of expanding his and Furness Railway's interests. By 1866 Schneider, Hannay and Ramsden had amalgamated to form the Barrow Hematite and Steel Co. Ten years later there were sixteen furnaces, producing up to 500 tons of steel. This was the pinnacle of Barrow's iron and steel industry, possessing the largest ironworks in the world.

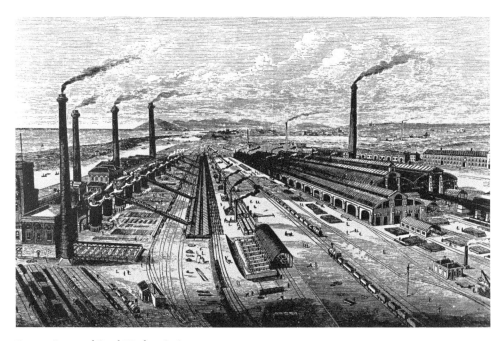

Barrow Iron and Steel Works, 1876.

With each blast furnace built at Hindpool came an influx of steel workers and blacksmiths from as far afield as Dudley and Birmingham. The Cornish flooded in at the time of recession in the tin mines and labourers were drawn from the rapidly growing Irish community. The boom time could not last forever and by the First World War the industry was flagging and so began a slow and painful decline. The final death knell came in 1963 when the ironworks closed with a loss of 700 jobs. The steelworks closed in 1984 and its passing was mourned despite the inevitability. Little is left to show for this massive industry, which seems incongruous when one considers it was one of the catalysts for Barrow's rapid growth and prosperity. The physical evidence is well hidden but is commemorated in the town at the Dock Museum and in artwork on Duke Street, but sadly little was done to preserve the buildings from this remarkable industrial history.

DID YOU KNOW?
The iron ore found in Barrow was a very high-grade Hematite, with high iron content and few impurities. Without the discovery of quality iron ore, the shipbuilding business would probably not have developed in Barrow.

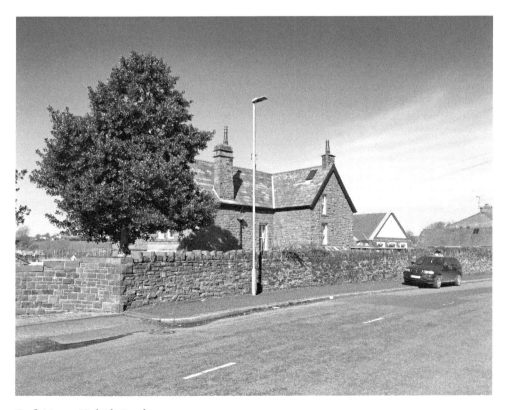

Croft Manor, Yarlside Road.

Evidence of the iron ore mines is scattered about the district and is easy to find if one knows where to look. At Yarlside there are many clues to the past. One of the most impressive is a magnificent sandstone house, which sits among 1930s semi-detached homes, along one of the old routes to Salthouse from Furness Abbey. It runs parallel to the railway line and the River Yarl. Croft Manor was built in the 1870s when the industry was at its peak. It is built on a grand scale with an extensive garden and outbuildings for a coach. The mine captain – an important man – lived there but it belonged to the Yarlside Mine, which was located north of this. The house has endured over the years with few external changes and has survived intact unlike many of the mine buildings. In the 1929 year book Mr A. Parkinson was resident there. Later a new house was built in the grounds in the 1980s on a much smaller scale, set back from the boundary wall and slightly out of place with the original.

The iron ore deposits were rich and of a good quality and the Yarlside and Stank mines grew, spreading across the landscape and providing more jobs for the miners who had migrated north when the Cornish mines closed. Schneider encouraged this, because of the expertise the miners brought with them.

Roose Village

The Cornish settled in Roose village, first mentioned in the Domesday Book, (Rosse) under the jurisdiction of Earl Tostig, the brother of Harold Godwineson. By the time of the Industrial Revolution it was principally a farming community and was little more than a hamlet.

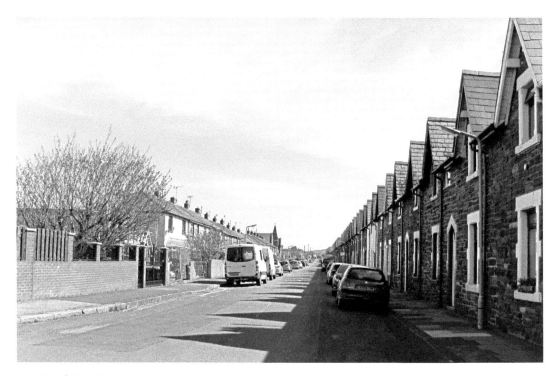

North Row, Roose.

However, it soon thrived, with purpose-built workers cottages and a railway line taking them to the mine head. The cottages are distinctive and have changed little over the years. The sandstone construction is sturdy and each cottage shared an entrance lobby. The terraces are in blocks, each house having a yard to the rear and opening onto a green, which once held the 'old line'. The track has gone but the old railway bridge towards the main line is still there, and the route can still be seen. The terraced cottages were built by the Hematite Mining Company in 1876–78. North and South Row have been added to with new houses being built to complete the streets and West Row was built after the Second World War as accommodation for police officers and their families. These have since fallen into private ownership and are separated from the old cottages by the wide main road.

Yarlside Mines

At Yarlside we can see evidence of the old workings and spoil heaps and ruined buildings. The most prominent feature is the hillside above Park House Farm. A huge scar of red clay is visible where the hillside collapsed and is a landmark noticeable for miles. The collapse occurred overnight in January 1915, and must have been a frightening experience for those working in the mine. Miners were aware of an impending catastrophe because of the movement of the timbers and prop shafts. The alarm went up and the miners evacuated. Apparently, the overseers suggested the miners retrieve as much equipment as they could before leaving. This was met with some derision and the miners left the mine as quickly as possible, without salvaging tools. This illustrates dangerous working conditions in the mines and there are many recorded accidents, some of them fatal. Conditions were harsh and hours were long, but the mines provided work and men and boys scrambled for jobs.

DID YOU KNOW?
The River Yarl is still known locally as 'Red River' due to the iron deposits in the clay washed into it, giving it a red colour.

Access to the mine workings at Yarlside was via a horse-drawn monorail originally. This was built by John Barraclough Fell in 1868 to transport the ore from Yarlside to the exchange wharf in Barrow for Furness Railway. Fell developed this further, replacing it in 1870 with an 8-inch narrow gauge rail system. By 1873 it had become a standard gauge railway. The old line is still visible below the bridge in the lane above Park House Farm. The old rail track follows the hillside and disappears into gorse bushes and is now a public pathway. Here many of the mine buildings have been removed completely or lie ruined and the land returned to agriculture.

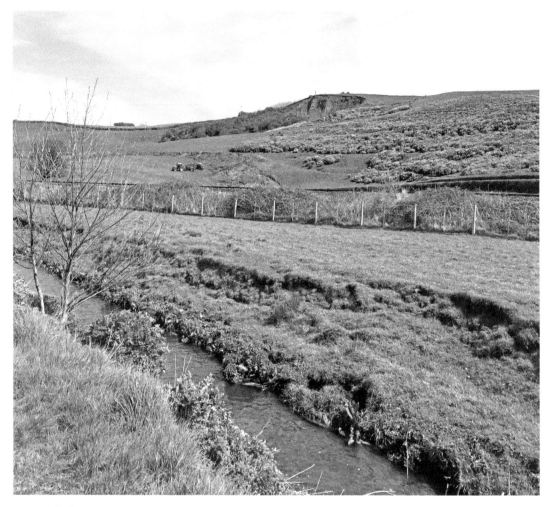

Yarlside Mines.

Stank Mines

A similar pattern of evidence is visible at Stank. Barrow Hematite Steel Co. owned mines including Park (output was 375,000 tons in 1872) and Stank. The scars on the land are permanent but their origin is easily forgotten. At Stank we see remnants of the mine buildings: Glenfield House was once the mining offices, built in 1875. The remains of the Ancillary Block, the gateway and mine entrance are still visible. Rose Cottage was once a mine lodge for managers and is little changed from the outside. Set further back from the road is the old engine house, probably the most iconic monument to the past. Some of these buildings have been in use as private dwellings ever since and most of them are constructed from locally quarried sandstone in keeping with the much older village they sit within. The places where the railway line cut through the landscape are now disappearing, apart from the two large piers of the railway bridge over the lane, which stand as a sentinel at the edge of the original village.

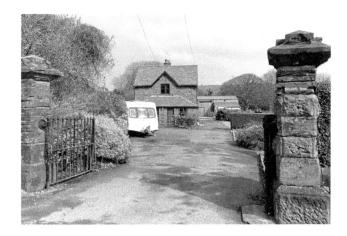

Glenfield House, Stank.

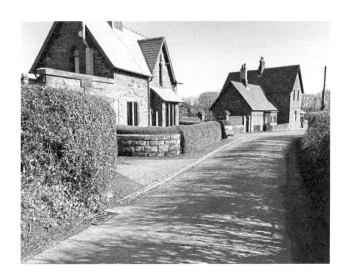

Rose Cottage, Stank.

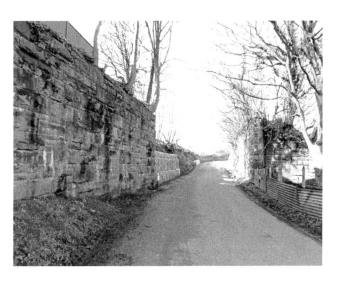

Railway bridge, Stank.

Lindal, Mouzell and Askam

Other mines workings are identifiable along the A590 to Barrow as it cuts through Lindal. Strange hills and bumps litter the fields, all man-made and derived from spoil from the mining process. Mouzell and Askam have similar detritus but one impressive relic is Askam Pier. This is constructed from slag from the steel process and endures the constant pounding by the Irish Sea. Elsewhere the remains of slag banks and ponds are now wildlife sites and the memory of the industry is only captured in the names of some of the streets, which grew in the nineteenth century to accommodate the growing workforce. Such names as 'Steel Street' are self-evident, others recall the names of those involved in the industry like 'Crossley' and 'Sharp'. As in Barrow, the rich seam of ore had run out by 1918 and most of the buildings associated with iron and steel had gone by the early 1930s.

The Depression in the 1930s harmed small villages such as Askam and there was little work, so enterprising citizens created opportunities to earn money, such as selling fish, or doing odd jobs and making things to sell. A centre was set up for the unemployed as a charitable institution at Yorke House (named after the charity in London) off Duddon Road. The unemployed men renovated the building and created a centre to benefit them and their families. There was a library, entertainment and other amenities. The unemployed families were provided with special gifts of things like Easter eggs and Christmas presents and they even had their own newspaper, The *Askam Echo*, which cost a penny, which went towards the building of the centre. Later, new industry grew in Askam such as the K-Shoe factory, which was a significant employer. This, too, has now gone and little remains to show it was ever there.

The largest and most prevalent remainder of the iron ore industry is, of course, the large slag bank facing Walney Channel. There has been some attempt by the council over

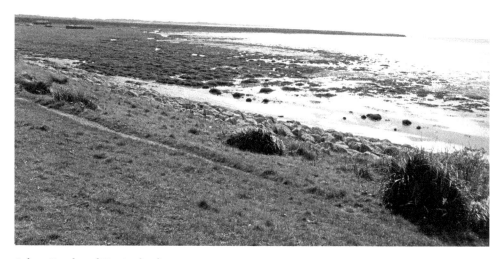

Askam Beach and Pier in the distance.

the years to reduce the size of this and landscape what remains. This has been partially successful as the removal of slag, for hardcore in building and road making, reduced the size. The formidable 'mountain' is much smaller than in the last century, but it is not easily disguised. It now forms part of a walk stretching along the channel from the Dock Museum. It is named Redman's Way, which is a nod to the red colour of the dust and mud that covered the miners. A statue was placed at the start of the walk, but sadly this was destroyed and all that remains is the base. The view from the top is spectacular, but looking at the bank from Walney, one can still identify this as industrial waste. The surrounding area would have looked very different in the nineteenth century, with tall chimneys and factories pumping out smoke and pollution.

Along Walney Road, the visitor captures this view of the dying remnant of the iron and steel industry. The extensive steelworks and foundries are all gone, replaced by modern commercial outlets, but here and there one catches a glimpse of the past. A lone wall runs along the road opposite the Asda store, the only surviving element of the steelworks, the rest swept away and hidden completely.

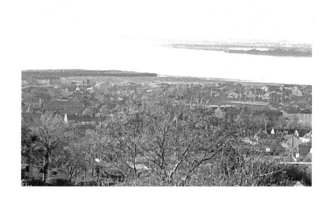

Askam village from Ireleth.

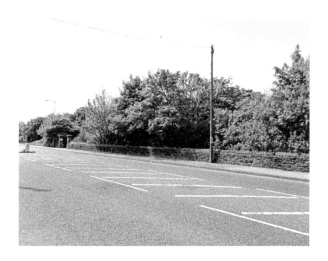

Steel Works Wall, Walney Road.

3. Ancient History: Swords, Hoards and Treasure

Barrow, of course, did not magically appear in the 1840s. It has a long and interesting history prior to the industrial revolution, not as a significant settlement, but as a wider district. Barrow as a habitation was small and fairly insignificant. Settlements had appeared across the peninsula and there is early evidence in places like Biggar and other places further afield, like Urswick Stone Walls and Birkrigg.

Dr G. Jackson carried out surveys at Walney Island in the 1960s and traces of human activity in prehistoric times at the North End were discovered. Evidence was fragmentary and probably only represents a small portion of what once existed. The paucity of finds and evidence of detritus left behind by early settlers possibly indicates the hunter-gatherer nature of their existence. Settlements would be temporary because of the nomadic lifestyle and artefacts widely spread instead of concentrated in one place. Much of Dr Jackson's work is unpublished so reference to this is generic rather than specific.

DID YOU KNOW?
The oldest recorded 'northerner' was discovered in a cave at Kent's Bank Cave, excavated by Chris Salisbury and other archaeologists around 1990–2001, and the bones are housed at the Dock Museum Barrow.

Although settlements have not been identified in this area, other evidence that supports early human activity has. Evidence of early exploitation of the iron ore in Furness at Urswick Walls has been found and this is also backed up my numerous prehistoric finds across the district. Bowden states that hematite staining on one of a pair of polished Langdale axes, high-status objects, provides evidence for this early exploitation of the prized iron ore. Numerous axes and tools have been discovered across Barrow-in-Furness and some of these are deposited at the Dock Museum. These finds would not be here if there was not at least a transient population of prehistoric people.

In Gleaston, an archaeological investigation was undertaken in the early 1990s. There are suggestions of a Mesolithic settlement and a lake in the valley. There seems to have been constant habitation from the Middle Ages and it is possible that this was an attractive place for the early hunter-gatherers to use. Firm evidence of habitation is elusive, mainly because of soil conditions and preservation, but there have been a number of flint and chert fragments, blades, bladelets and projectile points found during field walks and the excavation.

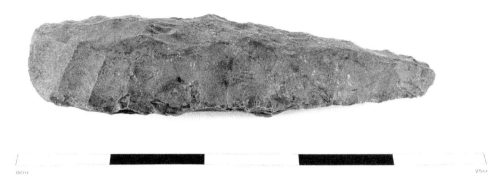

Langdale axes – rough out. (Courtesy Dock Museum)

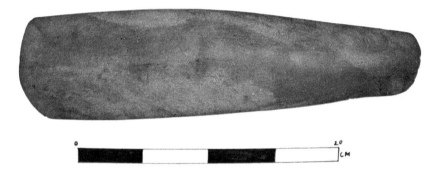

Smooth Langdale axe. (Courtesy Dock Museum)

A number of Bronze Age finds have been discovered, but again no settlements. One of the most significant is that at Roosecote in 1810. Farmers cleared away a tumulus revealing grave goods and urns containing cremation ashes. Other such burials have been found at Birkrigg, which although in Furness, is beyond the reach of the Barrow boundary. This period marked a transition from a nomadic lifestyle to small settlements. The evidence for this in Barrow is limited, but a probable settlement is Black or Back Castle, or the Cenotaph Hill in Barrow Park. Small finds have been found in abundance indicating a settlement. Further burials were found at Butts Beck, in Dalton in 1874, exposing high-status objects such as a bronze spear and sword suggesting a warrior or chief's burial. These finds assure us that the area was inhabited at this time, and hopefully one day a settlement may be revealed to add to our knowledge.

For many years there has been academic dispute about the level of influence on the area by the Romans. It was thought that they simply overlooked or ignored Furness as a place to settle. However, there have been some interesting finds that indicate there were trading links established with the rest of Roman Britain. There have been numerous discoveries of Roman coins scattered across the district in recent years. A magnificent Roman bracelet was discovered in 2012 by a metal detectorist in Dalton. It dates from the second or third century AD when Britain was under Roman rule. This silver bracelet

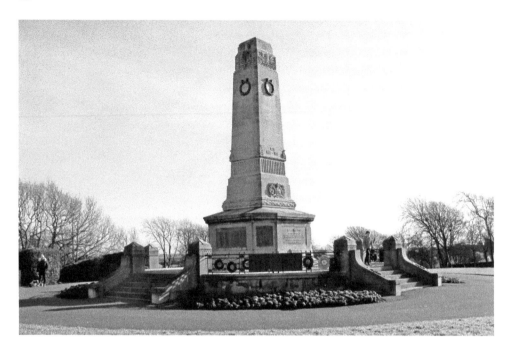

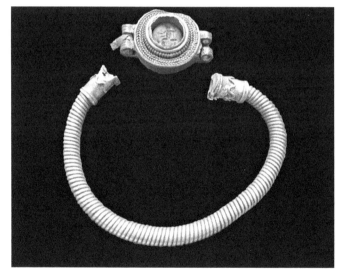

Above: Black Castle or Cenotaph Hill.

Left: Roman bracelet. (Courtesy Dock Museum)

is in the care of the Dock Museum, who raised the funds to purchase the artefact. It has a twisted hoop and hinged bezel, with a gem stone. The image of a seated Jupiter wearing a wreath, draped clothing and holding a sceptre is engraved on the stone. Jupiter is the most important Roman God in Roman mythology. In this depiction he holds a patera above a flaming altar. Some years previously, another unusual item was found near to Furness Abbey. This was a small statuette of the hero Hercules, the son of Jupiter. This too indicates Roman influence, if not a Roman presence in the area. The

Roman occupation must have had an indirect effect on Furness, especially considering the settlements and outposts at Lancaster, Ambleside, Ravenglass and Hardknott. The Brigantes tribe might have reached an agreement with Romans to co-exist and engage in trade and commerce.

A similar situation arises when looking for evidence of Viking occupation: there is a lack of tangible buildings evidence. However, it would be unlikely if the Vikings had not made incursions into Furness. Indeed the name Barrow allegedly derives from '*Barrai*', a Norse word, as do the names Fugl-ey (Foulney), Ro-ey (Roa) Byggergh (Biggar) and Rampside (Hrafns Saetr). Traditionally, being so close to the Lake District, where it is certain that the Norsemen raided and eventually settled, it would be unlikely that the rich agricultural land and natural harbours in the Furness Peninsula would be ignored. Further into Furness, of course, there is evidence of Norse building materials, for example the tympanum at Urswick Church. However, the discoveries at Rampside church support the idea more emphatically.

DID YOU KNOW?

The last 'arval' funeral took place in Dalton-in-Furness? An arval or arvol funeral has its origins in Norse culture. A meal of bread, cheese and ale was provided at the funeral house. Following the burial the mourners were then directed to an inn or hostelry. Here each group of four was served two quarts of ale, the cost being borne equally by the mourners and the person holding the funeral. The guests were then served with arval cake to take home to the women and those unable to attend. The final arval funeral in the town was of farmer William Jackson, who died on 25 February 1849.

Around 1854 the gravedigger William Jackson discovered a dagger approximately 30.5 centimetres in length and 2.5 centimetres wide. Its condition was very corroded, indicating many years under the soil. It had a tang without a pommel and a straight guard approximately 7 centimetres long. Unfortunately, this item was lost and its existence was only confirmed by Mr Jackson and his grandson.

A more substantial and verified find was made on 4 March 1909 by the sexton of Rampside church, Mr Jacob Helm, and his son Thomas. They were digging the grave for Thomas Curwen, the Trinity House pilot of Piel, when they unexpectedly discovered an ancient weapon. The sword was heavily corroded and was broken by Thomas when attempting to straighten it. When new it was around 84 centimetres in length, with a tang and pommel in the Viking style. It is unusual in that it only had one edge. The guard was rectangular and no workmanship was visible due to the level of corrosion and concretion. Unfortunately, in the intervening years the sword has suffered greatly and is now reduced to a disappointing lump of rusted iron. It is housed, but not on display, at the Dock Museum, sadly too damaged to be retrieved.

A more successful find is housed at the Dock Museum and forms the centrepiece of the Viking Gallery display. The Furness Hoard found in 2011 contained a medium-sized collection of Viking/Anglo-Saxon coins, ingots and silver pieces found in the Dalton-in-Furness area. It is from the later part of the Viking period, *c.* AD 959. The discovery of this hoard came shortly after the famous Silverdale Hoard was found and brought evidence of Viking occupation or influence within the Furness Peninsula. It is on permanent display at the Dock Museum, Barrow-in-Furness, purchased with funds raised from public subscription and donations.

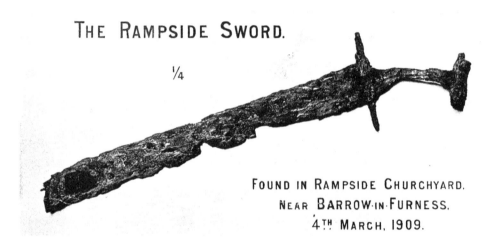

THE RAMPSIDE SWORD.

¼

FOUND IN RAMPSIDE CHURCHYARD.
NEAR BARROW-IN-FURNESS.
4TH MARCH, 1909.

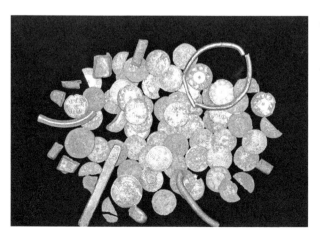

Above: Rampside sword. (Courtesy CWAAS)

Left: Furness Hoard. (Courtesy Dock Museum)

4. Medieval Memories: Castles, Abbeys and Granges

Aldingham and the le Flemings

Including Aldingham in *Secret Barrow* is stretching the Barrow-in-Furness boundary to its limit, but it would be remiss not to do so. An Anglo-Saxon settlement or vill is mentioned in Domesday and was held by Ernulf, a Saxon. The transfer of land from the Anglo-Saxons to Norman overlords was gradual but significant. The shift in the power base reminded the people who was in charge. Insurrection was dealt with swiftly and cruelly, much of the north being laid waste in a 'burnt earth' action – this was known as the Harrying of the North. Norman barons were rewarded with land and they staked their claims by building fortifications as a demonstration of power. Aldingham is probably built on the location of the original settlement, but the power base was further along the coast. This was the manor belonging to the Norman lord Michael le Fleming. It defined the boundary between his estate, named 'Muchland' in the Domesday Book, and that of Stephen of Boulogne and Mortain (later King Stephen). These lands were rich farming land and had belonged to Earl Tostig, King Harold's brother, but due to bad governance this had been removed and given to Earl Morcar. There was some depopulation and anarchy from the time of the conquest in 1066 onwards, and land was left uncultivated and uncared for.

The Aldingham motte is a mile to the west of the church and was originally a ringwork built by Roger the Poitevin before 1102. This was part of the redistribution of land by the Normans after the conquest. The mound and ditch was built by the le Flemings and is typical of a Norman motte and bailey. The cone-shaped motte had a wooden palisade at the top and would have been visible for some distance. This structure was a statement of power, a small fortification and a probable centre of administration. It struck the boundary between Muchland and Furness Abbey; lands were redistributed and after a few exchanges of land the manors were set.

The motte has been excavated and surveyed on a few occasions. An excavation was undertaken in the 1840s by the Cumberland and Westmorland Antiquarian and Archaeology Society when human remains were found. It was at first assumed that this was a burial mound, but more recent surveys have not supported this theory. Shards of pottery were found in 1968 when Brian Davison excavated a trench through the mound and he was able to date them to the early twelfth century. He suggested that the motte was unfinished and had three phases of building and it was added to with a rampart palisade and ditch. The fort was extended and developed but was eventually abandoned in favour of a new site at Gleaston. The mound is currently very vulnerable due to coastal erosion and it cries out for further excavation and survey. The settlement appears to have had an entrance to the bailey from the coastal side, which is a clear indication of how much the coast has eroded. There was possibly some kind of pond, maybe to store fish for

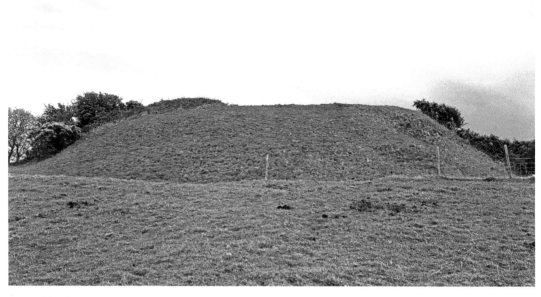

Aldingham Motte. (Picture N. Jepson)

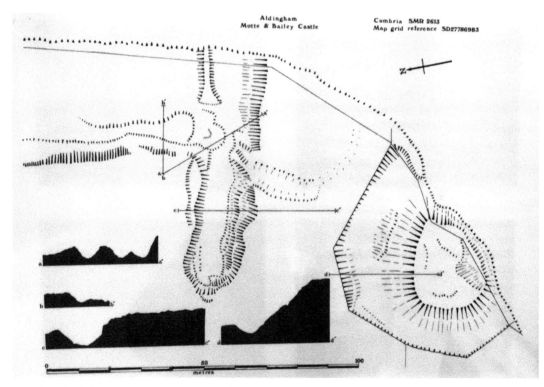

Geophysical survey. (Courtesy N. Jepson)

the inhabitants; however, there are indications that the pond ditch was also part of the fortification. In a geophysical survey in 2007 areas of high resistivity were recorded on the top and slope of the mound; further investigation of these could give a fuller picture of the fortification.

The le Flemings abandoned the motte and built a manor house, probably fortified, at Gleaston. In 1297 John de Harrington, a direct descendant of Le Fleming, began construction of the castle. Most likely the fortification was undertaken because of the threat of Scottish incursions. Raids were frequent, and were particularly devastating in 1316 and 1322. Work continued and the building was completed in 1340. It was a stone-built castle with a curtain wall. Its condition is very poor and it is in a dangerous state of repair. Its less-known claim to historic fame is through the families whose hands it passed. It eventually passed through marriage to Sir Thomas Grey, who was great-great-grandfather of Lady Jane Grey, the 'nine days Queen'. Local legend has it that she visited the castle, but this is not corroborated. From there it devolved to the Preston's and then the Cavendish family. It is now in private hands and is in the centre of a working farm.

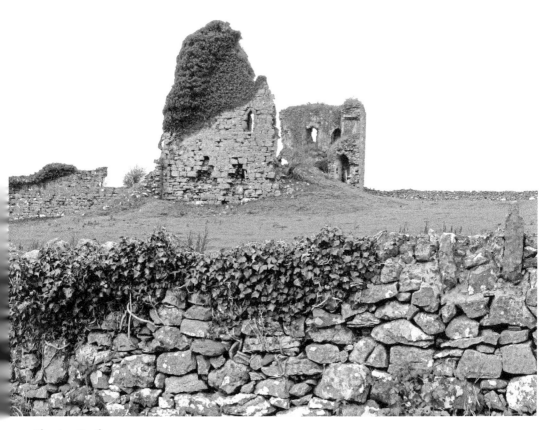

Gleaston Castle.

The Abbey of St Mary of Furness

Furness Abbey was a hugely influential and very rich Cistercian abbey and was a prime target for dissolution in 1537. The king's officers, under the direction of Thomas Cromwell, moved into the abbey destroying the icons and religious artefacts to prevent use as a religious building, removing goods and valuables, and finally pulling down the roof and walls. This was the first large abbey to undergo the process and they did a thorough job, leaving few artefacts for later generations to discover. Therefore, it was a revelation in 2010 when, during work to stabilise the foundations in the presbytery, an amazing discovery was made.

DID YOU KNOW?
Furness Abbey is allegedly haunted by a headless monk on a horse and a white lady mourning her lost love.

The skeleton of an abbot with his crosier and ring was discovered around 1.5 metres down, alongside numerous other bodies. The abbot was revealed to be between forty and fifty years old, approximately 5 feet 7 inches tall and his bones showed evidence of DISH, a condition linked to obesity and type 2 diabetes, which indicates he had a rich diet. He also had arthritis in his knees, which could be as a result of the condition, or maybe because he was pious and constantly kneeling and praying. We know he had high fish content in his diet, which is not really surprising considering the proximity to the sea. He must have been very important to be buried so close to the high altar, but at present it is impossible to identify him.

His crosier is a reworked twelfth-century piece made of gilded copper, with gilded silver medallions depicting the Archangel Michael defeating a dragon. The crook is decorated with a serpent's head. His ring was probably a penance ring because it has a point behind the stone, which would have been uncomfortable to wear. This was to remind him of his 'opus dei' or his duty to God. There might be a space behind the semi-precious stone for a small relic; however, this must remain conjecture as it would be too damaging to take it apart.

This find, made by archaeologists from Oxford Archaeology North on behalf of English Heritage, was unexpected and came at a crucial time for the abbey. The finds were said to be the most significant in the last fifty years and have done much to elevate the profile of this largely forgotten abbey. The story was reported nationally by *Channel 4 News* and other channels. It remains the highlight and centre of the exhibition and is a welcome enhancement to an already remarkable abbey.

Hidden from view within the abbey are many other pieces of the historical jigsaw. It is recorded in the Coucher books (two volumes of abbey history and business written in 1412 by Brother John Stell) that two Bishops of the Isles are buried here and even more importantly King Reginald (Rognvaldr Gudrodarson) of the Isle of Mann.

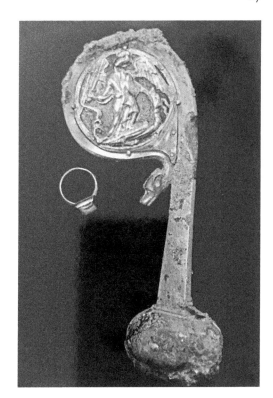

Right: Crosier and ring. (Permission English Heritage)

Below: Presbytery Furness Abbey. (Permission English Heritage)

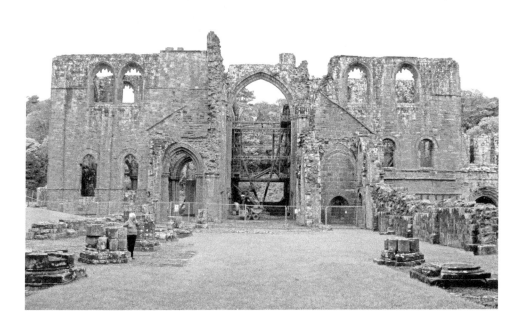

Their exact location is unknown and they might have been prey to the post-dissolution grave robbers. The likely place would be the nave of the church and other lesser nobles, such as knights and donors to the abbey, were also buried here, and there are a number of grave covers housed in the museum. A broken grave cover inscribed with the name Adam de Greenhaume (Grisholm) was found in the excavation in the presbytery. We know little about him but he must have been a donor to receive burial within its walls. Greenhaume was an abbey grange and the name still exists in a small farm and hamlet between Dalton and Askam.

DID YOU KNOW?
A medieval mason's mark appearing at Furness Abbey also appears at Fountains Abbey in Yorkshire.

The quarries from which the monks from Furness Abbey sourced their stones are located at various points around the abbey. The valley is long and narrow and the abbey has been slightly stretched to fit. What we see today is only part of it. The valley was perfect because it had the resources necessary to build a huge monastery. On the western edge of the valley is the best-preserved quarry, but hidden by trees, it is no longer obvious. The sandstone rock face stands proud among trees in a small wood. The main track where the stones would have been moved along is visible down to the lane. On closer inspection the mason's chisel marks are visible on the sandstone and random blocks are strewn around. It is fascinating to discover carved faces – now fading – hewn into the rock face, a mason's joke maybe or honing his skills. This quarry is fascinating and evocative of the great creativity of these long-dead masons.

At the head of the valley the locally named 'amphitheatre', a second quarry, is found. The valley opens up here and a natural bowl shape has emerged. Ridges, which give the area its name, run round the hillside ending at another small wooded copse. These are what remain of the sledge runs, which were used to transport the stone on wooden sledges pulled by oxen. The quarry is inundated with trees and shrubs and evidence of its origins is hard to find now.

A third quarry is more prominent, but not automatically recognisable as such. This is located behind the Abbot's Lodgings. This was originally the first infirmary, which as the abbey grew in size, was replaced by the larger one to the west. The building is unusual because its upper floor would have overhung the lower rooms and was built into the natural sandstone wall of the hillside beneath Abbotswood. Behind the building and along the hillside the quarry is evident – tool marks can be seen. The sedimentary layers in the rock face can be matched with blocks in the infirmary area, showing where these were sourced. The sandstone is a soft pink rock, which in some areas of the abbey has been gravely eroded and weathered. However, the sandstone endured for centuries, most of the damage probably arising from industrialisation and the resulting pollution.

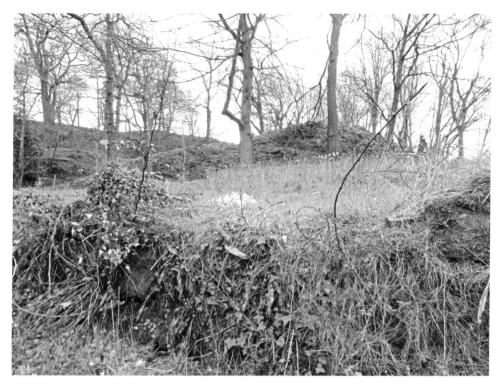

Site of Furness Abbey quarry.

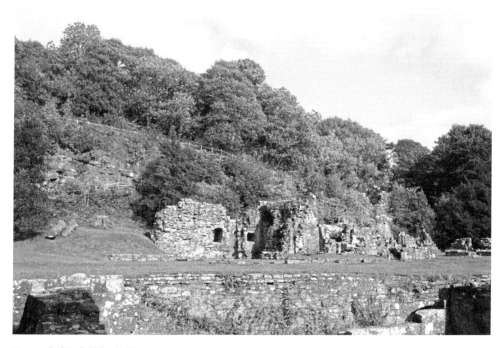

Quarry behind Abbot's House.

Dissolution

The constant litigation of Abbot Bankes had plunged the once prosperous abbey into debt and, unfortunately, this played into the hands of Thomas Cromwell, whose master plan for dissolution was about to unfold. Roger Pele, the final abbot, was a complete opposite to the arrogant and bombastic Bankes; he is often portrayed as weak and compliant, but in some ways he was a dupe, ripe for manipulation. He had been at Chancery in London, and Cromwell knew him well. His nomination to the abbacy of Furness was a poisoned chalice. It had come to the crown's attention on a number of occasions over land disputes, customs disputes and it was the second most prominent Cistercian monastery after Fountains, with massive land holdings.

A stream of correspondence and payments flowed from Pele to Cromwell, usually asking for help and assistance in his management of the abbey lands. The monastic community were split, many of them disliking Pele for his association with Cromwell. The wheels were set in motion for the suppression of the large abbeys and even though Furness paid bribes to high-ranking people at court, including Cromwell.

DID YOU KNOW?
Furness Abbey was the second largest and influential abbey after Fountains and the first large abbey to be dissolved by Henry VIII.

The commissioners were sent to inspect the state of the larger abbeys and their moral rectitude and at the end of 1535 Thomas Holcroft visited. The abbot and three monks were accused of immorality, but no great evidence was produced to declare the abbey totally corrupt. A friar called Robert Legate had been placed in the abbey to preach to the brothers, but essentially he was a spy for Cromwell and the Crown. He regularly reported misdemeanours back to the Crown and the most persuasive evidence was the deposition that Henry Salley had said 'it was never a good world since secular men and knaves had rule upon them and the King made Head of the Church.' This was damning enough, but compounding this was the knowledge that additionally to much treasonous talk, monks had joined the Commons (insurgents) from Cumberland at the rallying point at Swarthmoor.

True to form, Roger Pele was expedient and made his way to Rampside to escape by boat to meet with the Earl of Derby at Lathom. This abandonment of his post left the abbey in the charge of the prior – the bretheren were split in their loyalties. The vicar of Dalton was approached and the rebels wanted him to declare on their side. The vicar was as slippery as Pele, escaping to the woods and avoiding any involvement. The cellarer Michael Hammerton, the monk John Green and two monks of Furness joined Gilpin and handed over more than £23 to the rebel cause. The abbey tenants had been roused, though to be fair not all rose to the call. This insurrection was one of the deciding factors in dissolving the abbeys and the die was cast.

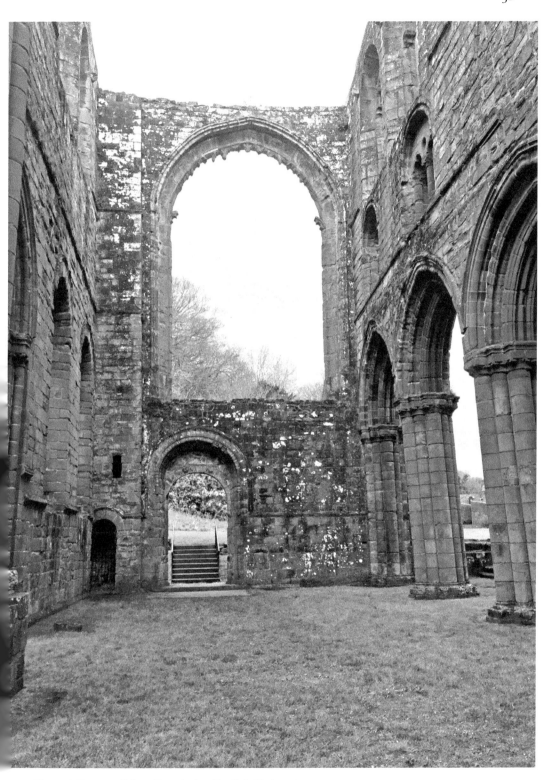

Chancel, Furness Abbey. (Permission English Heritage)

The monks were very lucky to escape with their lives; others such as the canons and yeomen of Cartmel were hanged for their disobedience. Three monks were imprisoned at Lancaster but not executed. The deed of surrender was signed by the abbot and his monks in the Chapter House at Furness on 9 April 1537. The remaining monks were punished for their disloyalty by receiving only 40s, out of which they had to buy secular clothing instead of pensions. One wonders what became of them. Pele himself was made vicar of Dalton, presumably at the expense of the current incumbent. The harsh treatment of the monks was remarked upon by the Earl of Sussex, who was the agent empowered with dissolving the abbey. He declared that 'the Furness Monks had been of as evil hearts and minds as any other.'

The other laymen, masons, and servants were paid until midsummer and let go. They probably hoped that they would be employed by whoever took over the abbey farms and lands and would face a time of uncertainty and poverty due to the dreadful agricultural depression. The cloister school, once teaching up to a hundred boys, was closed and the boys sent home. The almsmen who resided in the abbey were paid and sent away, but the eight poor widows supported by the monks were left without alms. The abbey had provided a safety net for the poor, the sick and the destitute, but this ended abruptly with the dissolution. The impact across the country would bring Poor Laws into being and made life very harsh for those unfortunate enough to fall on hard times.

Chapels and Churches

There was a small chapel in St Helen's Valley, between Dalton and Askam, which was under the jurisdiction of the monks at Furness Abbey. It was believed to be a chantry and is close to the St Helen's Holy Well, so it is possible there was a shrine there. There was some sort of construction at St Helen's farm but this was removed in the last century and placed in the vicarage cellar at Dalton and the stones numbered. The sandstone window, bricked up, is pictured in an earlier photograph of 1898, in situ at the farm. It is difficult to assess from the photograph whether the chapel is authentic, or if indeed the window has been reused in this building. Its current location is in St Mary's at Dalton where it has been pieced together and now stands as a small grotto at the back of the church. It would be interesting to see whether the mystery of this structure could be investigated more thoroughly, but as it stands it is a curiosity without any reliable context. The valley, named after St Helen, evidently had a natural spring, which was regarded as a Holy Well; this would possibly explain why a chapel was built close by.

There are reminders hidden in many places of the monastic history of Furness. One such item has hidden in plain sight for centuries. The font at Dalton Parish Church is evident in its link to Furness Abbey. Created from the same red sandstone as the abbey, it displays a carving of an abbatial crosier on one face of the font, which declares its significance to the abbey immediately. The font after the dissolution was removed and found its way to the churchyard, where it was left to brave the elements for many years. When the Victorian church was built it was decided to bring it inside the church, where it has remained ever since. It stands resplendent at the back of the nave and is a key feature of the church. Many children have been baptised in this font and it has proved its usefulness. This supports the close links the church had to Furness Abbey and the final abbot, Roger Pele, was given the living at Dalton following the destruction of the abbey.

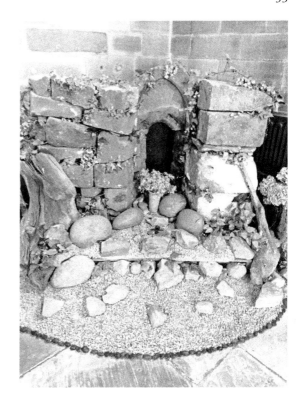

The remains of shrine from
St Helen's Valley.

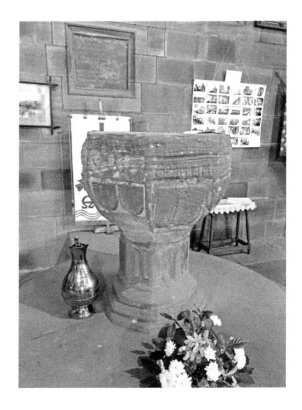

Font at Dalton Church.

Dalton Pele Tower

The Pele Tower at Dalton was built by the monks of Furness as a secure fortification against the Scots incursions in the fourteenth century. It became a judicial centre for the town and a gaol. The view of the castle has changed over the years and its appearance now is very different to when it belonged to the monks. Houses were built around it and the fabric of the castle became uncared for and dilapidated, the ground floor being used as a stable at one time. Many of the houses in Market Street are old; one which was the old Ship Inn bears the date 1683. The marketplace was remodelled in the nineteenth century and the ancient St Andrew's cross was replaced by the cross we see today. The stocks and whipping post were close to the gaol as one would expect. These were all removed in the later part of the century and in 1869 the fish stones were erected.

The fabric of the castle internally was completely remodelled. William Close in 1804 comments that the castle was in poor repair and describes many changes and alterations it had suffered to this date. The Duke of Buccleuch in the 1850s, who owned the castle, was responsible for many drastic changes, including the removal of some features and the addition of another staircase and fireplaces. The dungeon used to hold prisoners who were to appear before the court is still visible. This probably had an iron grille to cover the opening; it is very basic and would have been unpleasant.

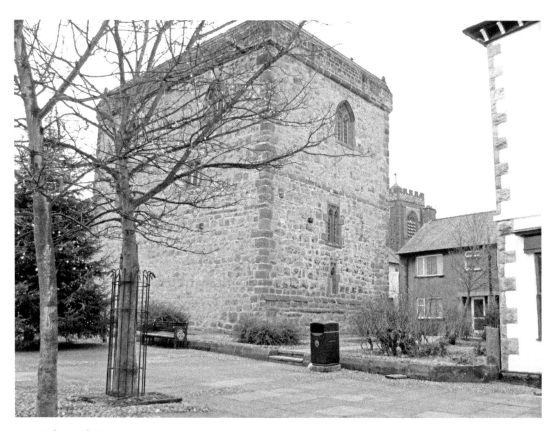

Dalton Pele Tower.

The castle is probably the second building on this site, the first possibly being destroyed during the Scot's incursion into Furness in 1316. Indeed, Furness was a favourite target for the Scots and in 1322 the Abbot of Furness, John Cockerham, met with Robert the Bruce, possibly at the castle, to discuss terms for peace. The result was the payment of a huge ransom by the abbot in return for safety of the Furness lands, which had been constantly raided and devastated over years. Bruce spent the night at Furness Abbey and the next day left to cross the sands to Lancaster, which was burnt and ransacked, before the Scots returned to the north.

The effects of the Great Raid were far reaching. The revenues reduced dramatically and the money sent to Rome to assist the building of St Peter's (Peter's pence) reduced from £8 to £2. Famine and disease followed the destruction of crops and the people suffered greatly, being in reduced circumstances for the next twenty years.

Items of interest now housed in the castle include some carved stone heads. Two of these are from the ruins at Furness Abbey following the dissolution. There is a carved head of a monk and one appears to be the image of Christ. Their state of preservation is good, probably because they were buried for so long. The third carving is more primitive and is probably Celtic in origin and may be a talisman to ward off evil spirits. These artefacts were discovered at Schoolwaters, Dalton, during the building of the housing estate.

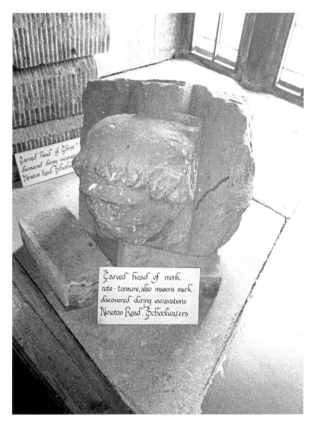

Carving of a monk at Dalton Castle.
(National Trust)

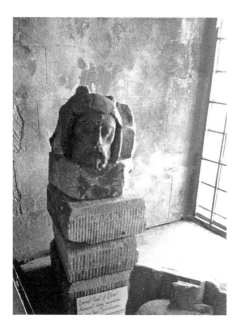

Carving of Christ at Dalton Castle. (National Trust)

The Pile of Fouldray

The medieval fortification at Piel, or the Pile of Fouldray, has found fame in a number of documentaries about heritage and is mentioned in many publications. The aspect most often focused on is the 'King of Piel' tradition. However, less well known is the possible reason that gave rise to the ritual.

On 5 June 1487 a young boy named Lambert Simnel landed at Piel with an army of Flemish, Irish and English troops. He was a pretender to the throne of Henry VII and was the puppet of ambitious men. His tutor Richard Simon saw a resemblance in this boy to the sons of Edward VI (better known as the Princes in the Tower), who had disappeared at the end of Richard III's reign. He groomed the boy and educated him, intending to declare him as Richard of York, the younger son. However, his plan changed when the young Earl of Warwick was rumoured to have died in the Tower. Warwick was another Plantagenet heir, the son of George Duke of Clarence. Simon manipulated the news and said that Warwick had escaped, attracting some Yorkist support.

Simnel was taken to Ireland where he was crowned at Dublin. Lord Kildare raised an army and was joined by the Earl of Lincoln and Viscount Lovell, aided by Margaret of Burgundy, the real earl's aunt. The army of mercenaries was led by Martin Swartz and they left Ireland to land at Piel. One local nobleman, Sir Thomas Broughton, joined this band of rebels. The army met with Henry's troops at Stoke where they were routed on 16 June 1487. Broughton, Lincoln and Fitzgerald were killed in battle, Lovell escaped and Simon, spared execution, was imprisoned. Kildare was granted a pardon. The poor boy at the centre of this debacle was pardoned because it was clear that this child had been used by his elders and had no power to resist the manipulation. He famously worked as a spit-boy in the royal kitchens, but later on he progressed to become a falconer. He appears to have led a life away from the intrigue of the court and politics and disappears from historical record.

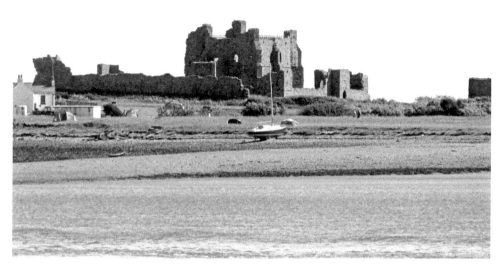

Pile of Fouldray.

The Lost Village of Sellergarth

The lost village of Sellergarth has an intriguing place in the historical record. Originally a grange belonging to Furness Abbey, Soler or Sellergarth grew to be a substantial holding. Initially it would have been worked by the lay brothers. These were monks who took holy orders, usually from the poorer and uneducated class. Although they took the same vows and prayed daily like the Quire monks or *monachi*, they were expected to perform their *opus dei* (work for God) in the fields, fisheries, forests and farms and were allowed out of the precinct. Gradually, the lay brothers diminished after the Black Death and granges were taken over by enterprising peasants, who were tenants of the abbey.

By the end of the sixteenth century Sellergarth was extensive and included the manor, Breastmill Beck and Rakesmoor Farm. The exact location of the village is unknown, though many have speculated it lies somewhere beneath Furness General Hospital or the surrounding fields near to Manor Farm. In December 1516 the monks, under the direction of Abbot Alexander Bankes, forcibly evicted the tenants and destroyed the village. This was to create parkland, New Park, for the abbot, and to fill it with deer for the pleasure of hunting. The abbot has a notorious reputation and even caused dissention in his own religious house. He was ejected by his own monks and Abbot John Dalton replaced him for a time. Bizarrely he managed to recoup his position and imprisoned Dalton and the monks who assisted him in the coup. The pope, however, had Dalton released, so one would assume that he had some sympathy with him.

Lawsuit followed lawsuit and Bankes appropriated lands from tenants for sheep pasture and parkland. The redoubtable William Case of Sellergarth litigated against this cruel and unjust action, saying it was his 'utter undoing'. The outcome of this legal action is uncertain, but we do know that tenants were forced to re-establish themselves in Newbarns, whose name is self-explanatory. The new settlement became a small village and has now become part of a larger suburb of Barrow. It is fascinating to see that some of the oldest houses in Barrow are situated here, probably replacing the original houses built after this relocation.

It is known that this kind of action informed some of the reasons and excuses for the Reformation. Even Sir Thomas More speaks of 'certain abbots' who 'leave no ground for tillage'; one cannot be sure he is speaking of Bankes, but he had probably heard of this disgraceful behaviour because of the significance of Furness Abbey.

A small but interesting footnote to this is that the descendants of William Case still live within the vicinity of the abbey and until recently 'tilled' the same land.

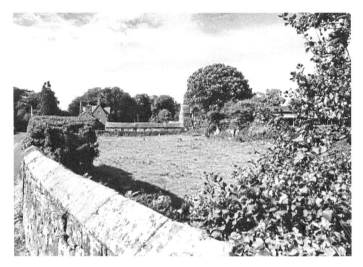

Manor Farm.

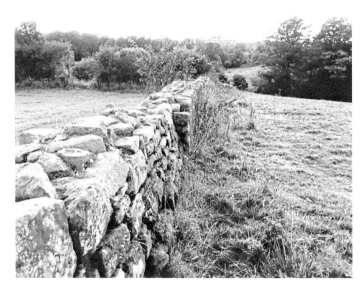

Precinct wall and valley where Sellergarth was possibly located.

Abbey Mills and Trackways

Furness Abbey had many holdings in their vast estates. There were at least three mills around the immediate site of the abbey, of which little or no evidence remains. However, if one looks closely enough, some evidence can be found. This indicates how important the abbey was in the infrastructure of the area and the level of control they had over it. Little Mill was located along the Haggs (the Low Road to the abbey from Dalton) and operated until the nineteenth century. This area was much disturbed during the development of the Furness Railway and though an old drawing remains, the building has all but disappeared. Walking along the Haggs (known as the Cistercian Way) some low walls remain and in the path is a well-preserved millstone.

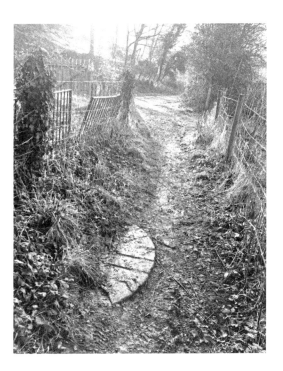

Millstone at the Haggs.

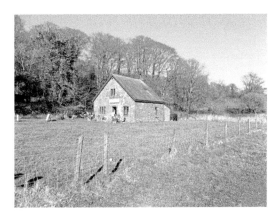

Abbey Mill.

Other mills were located at Roose and Orgrave. There is also a possibility of one mill at Bow Bridge. The river, though heavily realigned in the 1970s and disturbed by the railway in the nineteenth century, does appear to be a possible location for a mill race. The existing bridge is a fifteenth-century bridge, which would have been on one of the main packhorse routes from the abbey. This would have linked the abbey to New Mill, which was close by. The route is further supported by evidence found near the so-called Abbey Mill (now a café) in 2010, which is detailed separately.

Abbey Mill is now a small cafe, which is very popular with walkers and visitors to Furness Abbey. The official name is the Custodian's Cottage, but this was changed when it came under new ownership. Its particular charm lies in its great age and condition. Until recently it was the one remaining building with a roof timbers from the abbey intact (Wood, 1998). Sadly, a fire damaged the property in 1996 and a new roof was constructed. The original building dates back to the monastic times and would have been one of a number of ancillary buildings servicing the abbey. The building was adapted in the nineteenth century and it became the home of the custodian for the abbey. This in itself is significant because Furness Abbey, privately owned by the Furness Railway, and the Cavendish family, was a visitor attraction. The custodian was appointed by the company and was the first dedicated guide in England. The enterprise of the Furness Railway led to the abbey becoming a tourist destination and it was part of the excursion route for tourists to the Lakes including the abbey.

On inspection the whole building has sunk and the floor level internally is much higher than it was originally. The sandstone building retains many of its early features, and old doors and windows, now blocked up, can be seen. The new roof has compromised the stonework because it is possibly too heavy for the structure. This has caused some cracks to the walls and its metal frame is somewhat incongruous. The wooden beams inside are badly burnt and blackened but remain as evidence; when carbon dated before the fire, these were at least fifteenth century. This small section of the abbey precinct gives us a glimpse into the past and is remarkable having survived.

Sometimes change and development can reveal hidden treasures. This is true of the unexpected discovery in 2009 when a medieval trackway was uncovered by Oxford

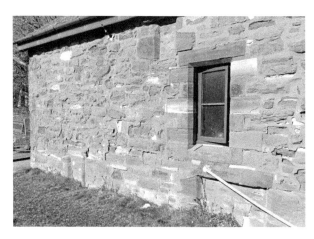

Abbey Mill showing the old door.

Archaeology North. A new Abbey Greenway cycle track was constructed by Cumbria County Council and because of the archaeological sensitivity of the area a watching brief was undertaken along its length. A cobbled track was found at the head of the path, 9 metres wide, running north-west/south-east. At the western edge there was a linear feature that might have acted as a kerb or edging. Slightly to the east were wheel ruts, which had damaged the cobbles. The track was not identified on OS maps, being further east than other tracks marked. This would suggest it was an earlier track, which had been replaced by a later one further east. The direction of the track appears to travel towards the railway line and beyond this is Bow Bridge, which was probably part of the packhorse route. This seems a logical assumption to make on the evidence available, however, further excavation would be required to confirm this as other features, such as the fish ponds, have not as yet been securely located.

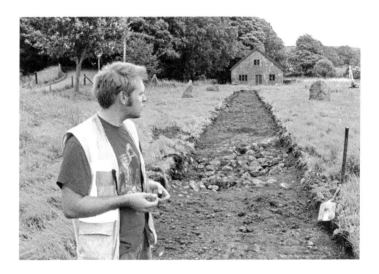

Old medieval road uncovered.

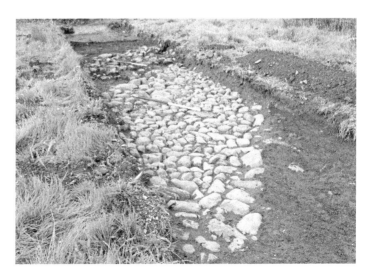

Cobbled surface of the road.

Most abbeys retained fishponds and it seems clear that Furness was no exception. There has been some speculation about their location, but with two becks running into the valley it would seem negligent if they had not utilised this opportunity. During excavations in the amphitheatre in the 1980s (the south end of the valley) Jason Wood identified possible sluices, which could indicate the position of the ponds. However, an alternative site could be further east in the field adjoining Bow Bridge. From aerial views there are depressions in this field, which could also be the remaining evidence for fish ponds.

Remnants of the monastic precinct walls are visible all around the abbey area. The wall stretches from the West Gate in Manor Road, following the ridge around the rim of the valley. The railway bisects it and then continues across the field near Bow Bridge. This portion leads across the fields towards Bow Bridge and would have reached 3 metres in height. The road breaks into it again but it resumes on the other side and is well preserved and quite high at this point. It encloses what would have been the abbey parkland, which was extensive, and meanders through Abbotswood, disappearing into Abbey Road. It can be picked up again, looking across to Manor Farm from Jubilee Bridge, where it connects once more with the West Gate. It is quite remarkable that this boundary still exists, but this is partly due to the walls being adopted by the farmers as field boundaries, albeit at a much lower height.

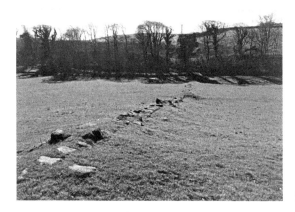

Remains of precinct wall.

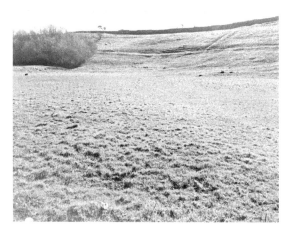

Precinct wall around the rim of the amphitheatre.

Abbey Granges were the method by which the monks controlled and developed the countryside. They were worked and managed by the lay brothers, who took holy orders but were given dispensation to work outside the confines of the precinct doing manual labour. These monks would return regularly to the abbey and report back to the grangiarius (the master of the granges), who in turn reported to the cellarer. The granges grew and some became small villages and hamlets.

The peasantry would contribute work to their feudal lord, who in this case would be the abbot of Furness. This would be in the form of week work, days dedicated each week to the abbey to work their land and granges, and boon work, which was extra days given at times like harvest or ploughing. This system also entailed giving crops or coin to the lord as payment for certain privileges, like selling animals or for renting land. The system kept the peasantry down and was often weighted towards the wellbeing of the lord.

One example of such work was recorded for the peasants of Walney, who in return for land usage had to ensure the upkeep of the dykes and sea defences on behalf of the monks. No doubt it benefitted the peasants too, but the monks were able to extract work and goods on the efforts of their peasants.

The abbey granges make up many of the small villages and settlements around the Furness area, Barrow (Barrai) being one – there were eight in all. Others at Roose (Rosse), Stank and Dendron are now villages radiating from the central point at the abbey. Some are less obvious, but the names still exist, such as Parkhouse, Greenhaume, Ireleth, Marsh Grange, Cocken and Sandscale. Wherever you are in the Barrow area you are never too far from an echo of the monastic heritage of Furness Abbey.

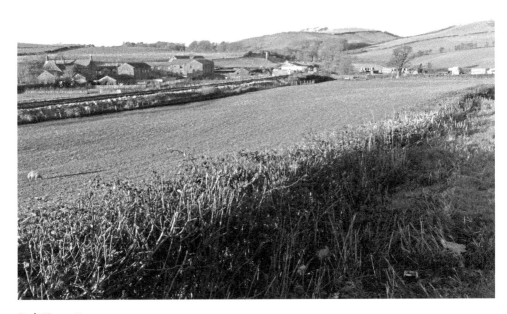

Park House Farm.

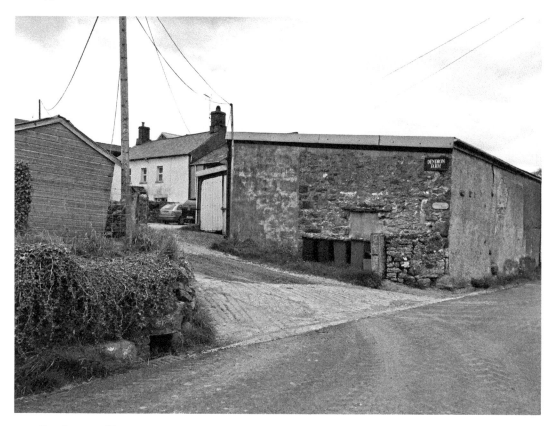

Dendron, an abbey grange.

Marsh Grange is known to have existed as early as 1252 and was originally named Stephengarth. Garth is another name for grange or farm and Stephen possibly refers to Stephen Count of Boulogne and Mortain, who gifted the land to Furness Abbey.

Following the dissolution it fell to Sir Hugh Askew. Margaret Askew was born here and she married Judge Thomas Fell of Swarthmoor in 1632. These two people were instrumental in welcoming George Fox to the area, which led to him establishing the Quaker movement. Judge Fell was supportive of Fox and his wife became a Quaker, and after Fell died she married Fox in 1669. Swarthmoor Hall has become the centre for the Quakers and welcomes them from all over the world.

5. Graves, Poets and Scholars

Barrow Cemetery

Barrow Cemetery was established in 1873 in response to the growing population of Barrow and recognising it was becoming a fully-fledged civic entity. Traditionally people had been buried at St Mary's, the parish church at Dalton, some may have been interred at the Walney chapel of ease and others at St Michael's Church, Rampside. This arrangement was adequate until the population rose rapidly during Barrow's industrial revolution, with families arriving in the town to find work. The infrastructure in the town was developing and many of the municipal facilities we take for granted were just not available. The town fathers and investors began to look towards making improvements and extending the limited utilities and services. Sanitation, health and overcrowding were major issues while the town was growing and the burial arrangements were totally inadequate. The route to the chapels was little more than a track and the registrar for deaths lived at Urswick, which was inconvenient for the residents of Barrow. A splendid municipal cemetery was planned on quite a grand scale. A parcel of land was offered to the town at a nominal price by the Duke of Devonshire and the municipal cemetery was created.

The long processional driveway led to the chapel at the top of the hill rising above the town and standing at the edge of Sowerby Woods. Sir James Ramsden himself would eventually occupy a splendid mausoleum at the summit, overlooking the town he had helped to create, even in death.

The cemetery was laid out following the hierarchy and prejudice of the day: Anglican burials closer to the chapel and top of the hill, Nonconformists behind and right at the back of the site the Roman Catholic section.

At the very top sat the graves and memorials of the great and the good – all Anglicans, naturally. They were allotted their own sections, which were in the most prominent positions, further from the gate and towards the summit of the hill. The less prosperous Church of England burials were lower down and further away from the worthies at the top, with smaller stones to mark the graves. The poor were in a large plot of unmarked graves, a large grass covered area is obvious as the hill drops away. These are common graves and would be for those unable to provide a marker; for example local workers who were not paupers but who would have no money to waste on memorials. Paupers' graves would also be unmarked.

The Anglican chapel, by design, was at the top of the drive on the summit of the hill. The original building was a grand Gothic construct and bears no resemblance to the current chapel and crematorium, another old building swept away in preference of modernity. The crematorium and chapel, first built in 1962, have recently been remodelled to allow for staff accommodation centrally, rather than at the gatehouse at the entrance to the cemetery. Prior to 1962 the people who wanted cremations were forced to make the long journey to Blackpool Crematorium.

The chapel was used for Nonconformist services too and their plot of land was set further back, but still in a fairly prominent place. The stones here tend to be simpler and have less overt ornamentation and religious imagery.

Finally, right at the back are the Roman Catholic graves, the positioning of these reflecting the status given in the nineteenth century to Catholicism. There was tension in the community at this time because of the disparity of wages, which were deliberately held down for Roman Catholics. There was prejudice and bigotry against the largely Irish residents, who were integral in creating the railway and the docks. Therefore, it is not surprising that the Roman Catholic population wanted a dedicated chapel of ease for their own use when the cemetery was built. This section is different to the other two already mentioned. The iconography of the stones proclaims the nature of the religion, with statues, crucifixes and other overt religious imagery. At the end of the cemetery stands a now derelict chapel for the use of the Roman Catholic community. It was raised

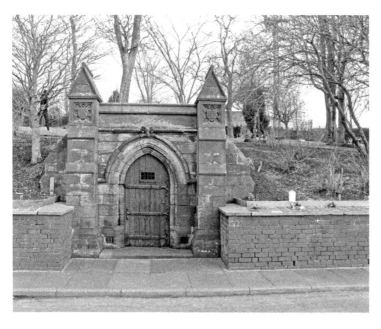

Ramsden's mausoleum.

by public subscription for the Roman Catholic population, but later, as cremation became popular, fell out of use.

Sir James Ramsden, the first mayor of Barrow and town father, has arguably the best plot in the cemetery. The Ramsden tomb, however, is almost forgotten and many people are unaware of its existence tucked away at the top of the drive, opposite the crematorium. His emblem of the ram is carved in sandstone over the entrance and the Barrow coat of arms flank it at either side. Its imposing, heavy studded wooden door has an open grille, tantalisingly encouraging the visitor to peer through. He resides with his wife Hannah, son Frederic and a gentleman friend. Although Fred was involved with many aspects of the town and its industry, he never made the same impact as his father. He never married and the Ramsden line died with him. The prominence of the tomb sets the levels of importance for the cemetery and other mayors can be found slightly below Ramsden. The area around the summit is full of high-status monuments of the great and the worthy and of course the rich.

Graves of the Good and the Interesting

There are a number of mayors and other town dignitaries buried in Barrow Cemetery, each jockeying for prominence and grandeur, clustering around the summit. Many of them have their own unique story to tell, but there are some very unexpected and unusual memorials of people one would not expect to lie in a northern industrial town.

One such grave is in the Roman Catholic section, a quietly understated monument until one reads the inscription proclaiming the resting place of Mary Countess de Rosetti and her husband Reno Pepi. This is unexpected and the story behind it is a moving one. Reno Pepi was a famous variety performer and quick-change artist. He was a music hall entrepreneur and was responsible for a number of theatres throughout the country,

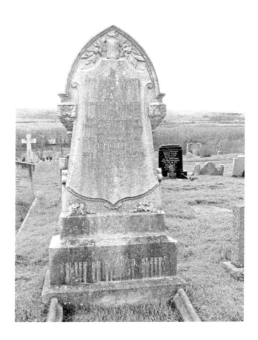

Rossetti grave.

including one in Barrow. Variety and music hall was very popular and a mass form of entertainment in the late nineteenth and early twentieth century.

Sadly, the countess died in 1915 while Signor Pepi was working at the theatre they had established in Barrow-in-Furness. Following her death Reno continued to develop his theatre business and left to work in the Darlington Civic Theatre. Reno died in Darlington in 1927 and his funeral was attended by 200 mourners at St Augustine's Roman Catholic Church. He is still remembered there and is reputed to haunt the playhouse. However, that is not the end of the story. He had left instructions to be returned to Barrow for interment. A funeral cortege brought him across the A66 back to Barrow-in-Furness to be buried next to his beloved countess, with a final flair for the theatrical, buried in full evening dress.

Oddly, yet another music hall artist, William Connor, is buried at Barrow. He resides in the Roman Catholic section and he was playing in Barrow at the time of his death in October 1880. He was known for his 'low comedy' and chair balancing and was a renowned 'negro delineator', which manifested as a comic black character called Lorenzo, who was popular at the time. He faltered on stage at the Star Music Hall during his balancing act and collapsed twice. It was assumed that the young man, who was thirty-two at the time of his death, was under the influence of alcohol but it was decided to take him home. He had previously complained of poor circulation and cold hands and was found dead at 8 o'clock the next morning.

He died in his lodgings at Crellin Street. The death was apparently sudden and unexpected and there was even a suggestion of suspicious circumstances. Dr Settle, who performed the post-mortem, however, stated that Connor had died from a blood clot on the brain. His grave stone declares that it was paid for by 'a few Manchester friends' – possibly other travelling performers like himself.

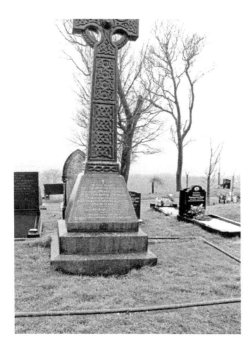

Caffrey monument.

A third important grave memorial in the Roman Catholic section is that of Father Caffrey. Caffrey was an Irishman and he organised food kitchens, clothes and blankets for distribution among the poor. In 1897 he invited the Sisters of the Sacred Heart of Mary, from Seafield Convent, Liverpool, to teach in the Catholic elementary schools and establish a convent school. The school at St Mary's was the forerunner to the two RC primary schools built in the 1960s at St Pius in Ormsgill and Holy Family in Newbarns. Caffrey's reputation is remembered not only in the memorial in the cemetery, which was subscribed to by his parishioners, regardless of their continuing poverty, but also in Caffrey Court, which stands where St Mary's Hall used to be.

Another little-noticed monument is that of James Gall. Unusual because it is a reproduction of the third Eddystone Lighthouse, Smeaton's Tower, this is a replica of Hoad Monument in Ulverston. The lighthouse was used in Ulverston to commemorate Sir John Barrow, who was a Lord of the Admiralty, born in Ulverston. In this case, however, it commemorates a very famous incident at the Longstone Lighthouse on the Farne Islands.

The memorial stands as testament to the bravery of Grace Darling, the daughter of the lighthouse keeper at Longstone, who braved the seas in a rowing boat to rescue sailors from the wreck of the SS *Forfarshire* in 1838. The sailor James Gall, who this monument remembers, was one of the survivors and was nursed back to health by Grace in the lighthouse. The memorial is poignant because Grace herself died in 1842, aged twenty-six, of tuberculosis but the man she helped to save lived on a full fifty-one years more because of her actions. Gall was a seaman all his life and was master of a Barrow ship, which is why he rests in the cemetery at Barrow.

Opposite the Pepi grave, set back is the grave of ex-professional footballer Walter John (Jack) Baggett. Not a native of Barrow, he is remembered fondly for his links with

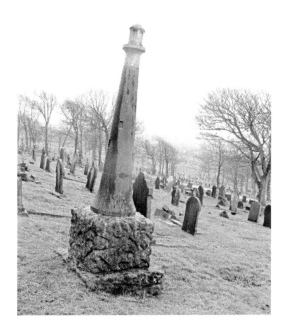

James Gall Monument.

Barrow AFC. He played for Wolverhampton Wanderers briefly, but did not make the first team and later played for Bolton Wanderers in the 1920s. He worked as a coach in the 1930s in Greece, Turkey and Cyprus. In 1941 he was forced to escape from the German forces in Greece during the Second World War. He moved to Barrow when they were in the Third Division North at Holker Street in 1954 and acted as physiotherapist, treating injuries and looking after the players. He died aged seventy-six in 1978.

Barrow Cemetery holds the grave of a holder of the Victoria Cross. This illustrious decoration was awarded to Private Samuel Wassall, who was attached to the 80th Regiment (Staffordshires) during the Zulu War in 1879. During a surprise attack on the camp at Isandhlwana, on the Tufela River, the majority of the regiment was massacred. Wassall was one of the few who escaped towards the river. His escape was impeded when he noticed a fellow soldier struggling for survival in the water. Without thought for his safety, he swam into the river and rescued Private Westwood under heavy enemy fire and managed to pull him to shore. He assisted him across the river, still under fire. The two escaped with their lives and Wassall became the youngest man in the British Army at the time to win a Victoria Cross, being only twenty-one years old.

In 1917 he was presented to the king at Furness Abbey station during a visit he made to the town. In 1920 he attended a reception at Buckingham Palace to meet the George V and Queen Mary. This first visit to London delighted him and he stated it was one of greatest experiences in his life. He was celebrated locally and often attended events such as the unveiling of the Cenotaph in Barrow Park in 1921. He frequently laid the wreath on Armistice Day and was much respected. He died at the age of seventy in 1927 and was afforded a full military funeral, with a guard of honour from the 4th Battalion King's Own. A firing party fired three volleys over the coffin at the cemetery and the Last Post was played by a bugler. His grave stone is emblazoned with the Victoria Cross and relates the story of his bravery.

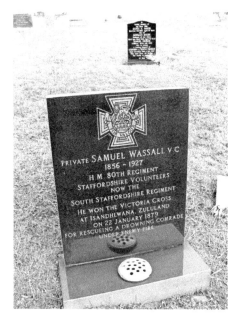

Grave of Samuel Wassall VC.

Poets, Artists and Writers

Although the Furness Peninsula was never as popular as the Lake District, there was acknowledgment that its heritage and natural environment were special. Wordsworth was a visitor to the area on numerous occasions. He is known to have visited Rampside at the end of the eighteenth century. The village had a reputation as a bathing resort and his visits to the seaside and the view over to Piel Island and Castle inspired him to write about it. Another favourite place of his was Furness Abbey and he wrote about it more than once, notably in his 'Prelude'. He wrote of the intrusion of the Furness Railway line, which ran through the back of the valley, close to the East window. He objected strongly and felt it was the wrong place to build a noisy railway. In 'At Furness Abbey' (1844) the lines resonate through the centuries and are as appropriate now as they were then.

> Here, where, of havoc tired and rash undoing,
> Man left this Structure to become Time's prey
> A soothing spirit follows in the way
> That Nature takes, her counter-work pursuing.
> See how her Ivy clasps the sacred Ruin
> Fall to prevent or beautify decay;
> And, on the mouldered walls, how bright, how gay,
> The flowers in pearly dews their bloom renewing!
> Thanks to the place, blessings upon the hour;
> Even as I speak the rising Sun's first smile
> Gleams on the grass-crowned top of yon tall Tower
> Whose cawing occupants with joy proclaim
> Prescriptive title to the shattered pile
> Where, Cavendish, 'thine' seems nothing but a name!

We can see from this work the 'Romantic' ideals of beauty and nature coming through strongly. He was an advocate of 'mouldered walls', overwhelmed by nature. He wanted the places he knew and loved to remain as they were, protected yet natural; one can only wonder at what he would think of the appearance of the abbey now. Certainly, it is not quite as manicured as it was in the twentieth century, but the brickwork is more exposed and visible. He would no doubt lament the trains still rumbling by every hour and would dislike the car park and abhor the visitor centre, but if he looked closely he would still see the abbey he loved.

DID YOU KNOW?

Chris Blackhurst, editor of *The Independent*, was born in 1959 and raised in Barrow-in-Furness. He was educated at Barrow Grammar School for Boys and Trinity, Cambridge. He has worked for the *Sunday Times*, *Sunday Express* and *Evening Standard*. He is an advocate of grammar schools based on his own positive experience at BGSB.

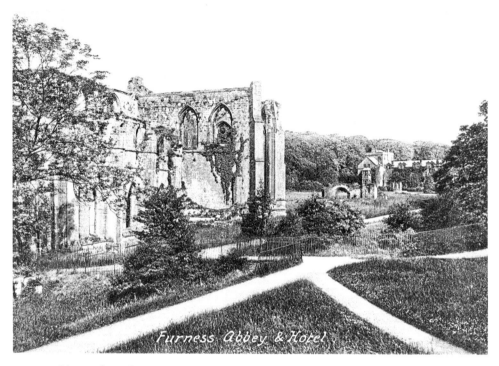

Furness Abbey and Hotel.

The reference to 'Cavendish' is the 7th Duke of Devonshire, William Cavendish. Cavendish owned much of the Furness Peninsula including Furness Abbey, which they inherited from the Preston branch of the family. In the early 1840s Cavendish funded a new railway to transport slate and iron ore to Barrow where it was shipped out. The proposal to build a railway through the Valley of Nightshade, in which the abbey sits, was an anathema to Wordsworth. He had fond memories of Furness as a youth and lamented the loss of peace and tranquillity. His anger was directed at the industrialist and financier of the project – in much the same way he attacked the 'villas', which were to be built by Manchester factory owners on the shores of his beloved lakes.

The second part of 'At Furness Abbey' (1845) refers to the railway construction next to the abbey and its labourers. This is a reflective piece and he noted that despite the rough and noisy nature of the navvies constructing the railway, they are affected by the spirituality of the abbey and behave in a respectful way. This is shown in the lines,

> They sit, they walk
> Among the Ruins, but no idle talk
> Is heard; to grave demeanour all are bound

He marvels at the reverence these 'simple-hearted men' show, but does not miss the opportunity to attack those he holds responsible for the desecration of the abbey: 'Profane Despoilers, stand ye not reproved'.

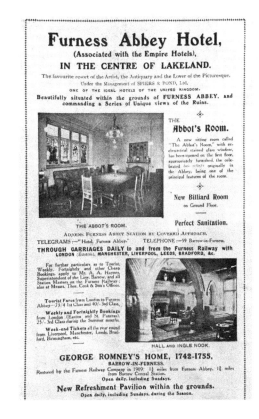

Advert for Furness Abbey Hotel.

The Romantic Movement was not just restricted to poets of course. The Grand Tours, popular in the eighteenth century, had become restricted during the Napoleonic Wars and alternative destinations were sought. The wilds of the untamed north seemed very attractive and drew interest from artists and painters alike. In 1797 J. M. W. Turner visited and sketched the abbey. There are a number of sketches remaining from the 'Tweed and Lakes Sketchbook', including the Chapter House, the Infirmary and the interior of the church. These are pencil sketches on white wove paper. They are easily identifiable as Furness Abbey, despite the changes to vegetation and some of the removal of walls. The lure for the artist is as strong now as it was for Turner – local artists can often be found sketching or painting.

Rupert Potter, the father of Beatrix Potter, spent many holidays in the area and photographed many well-known landmarks including Furness Abbey. The family visited the abbey on 13 September 1900 and Rupert and Beatrix photographed it extensively.

Dalton Parish Church

St Mary's Church stands in an elevated position near Dalton Castle. An earlier medieval church was swept away and a new one was designed by Austin and Paley, the respected Lancaster architects. The new church, built in the 1880s, retains a Gothic style and is as impressive as any of those built in the new town of Barrow.

In the small churchyard is a plaque in the memorial garden dedicated to victims of the Bubonic Plague during 1631–32, which devastated the whole country. The plague pit contains 360 victims, almost half the population of Dalton, buried together. The plague was brought to the town by Mr and Mrs Lancaster from London. The current memorial was dedicated in 1985 by the Dalton Civic Society.

In the graveyard, too, is a grave of George Romney, the artist who died in Kendal in 1802, but laid to rest here in the place of his birth. Although born in Dalton, he was brought up in a cottage in High Cocken in Barrow and went to school in the village of Dendron. He is one of the most important portrait painters of his time, comparable to Reynolds and Gainsborough. He painted many pictures of Emma Hart, later Lady Hamilton, Nelson's mistress, and was estranged from his wife and family while he made his fortune in London. He returned to them two years before he died and his forgiving wife nursed him. His memorial is in the quiet graveyard of the church and he is claimed by both Dalton and Barrow as a famous son.

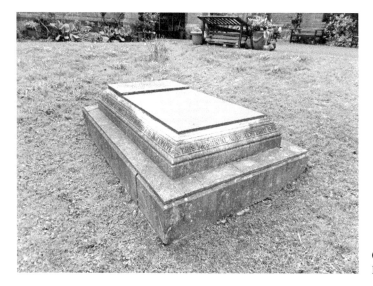

George Romney's grave, Dalton.

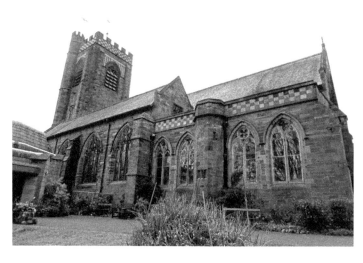

St Mary's, Dalton.

Villas, Tales and Historians

If Abbotswood was a temple to the Furness Railway Co. and the Duke of Devonshire, then Millwood was the same for the iron industry and the Duke of Buccleuch. Wadham was the mineral agent for Buccleuch and rose in a similar way to Ramsden. He had the manor built for Wadham, which was completed in 1860. He became involved in the same civic entities as Ramsden, becoming mayor of Barrow three times and a director of Furness Railway and Barrow Hematite Mining Co. Like Ramsden he was afforded his own railway siding at the bottom of his garden. There are still signs of this if one looks closely. This mansion luckily escaped the fate of Abbotswood and still exists. The view of it across the valley is still unimpeded and it sits resplendent in the trees. It has been separated into two dwellings nowadays but still retains some of its former grandeur.

The Wadhams lived there until the 1940s. During the Second World War the mansion housed German evacuees. Millwood became a retirement home in the 1950s until the 1980s, when it reverted to private ownership once again.

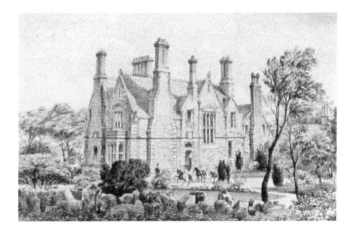

Millwood.

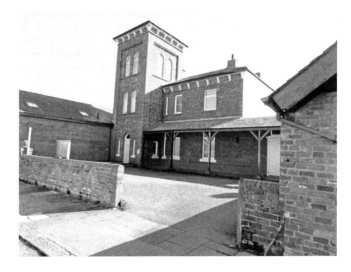

Villa Marina, Roa Island.

The third of the triumvirate of industrialists was H. W. Schneider, the iron ore speculator who was instrumental in harnassing the production and processing of iron ore in Furness alongside Ramsden. His principal home was at Belsfield in Windermere, but he owned two more closer to Barrow. One of these was the Villa Marina at Roa Island, overlooking Morecambe Bay towards Piel Island. The house after Schneider's day became a laboratory for the fisheries and later an army base during the Second World War.

DID YOU KNOW?

Barrovian Willie Horne, the English rugby league player, played for Great Britain, England, Lancashire and Barrow between 1943 and 1959, captaining all four teams. In 2014 he was inducted into the Rugby League Hall of Fame and is considered one of the best twenty-three players in the history of British rugby. His statue was unveiled close to Craven Park Rugby Ground in 2004.

Barrow and the Furness area has often been the inspiration for poets and painters, but how many people know that it was also the location for a series of children's stories? The famous railway stories by the Revd Wilbert Awdry were based upon real life events in Furness. One event was mentioned in the story called 'Down the Mine'. It tells of Thomas the Tank Engine (a really useful engine) who one day falls down a hole that appears on the track. The fireman and driver escape by leaping from the train but poor Thomas is stuck in the hole. Luckily, he is rescued by the big blue engine, Gordon, who hauls him out to safety. In 1892 an engine did indeed fall into a newly opened up hole, caused by an abandoned iron ore mine. As in the story there were no casualties and both the driver and fireman jumped clear. However, the train was not so lucky; there was no big blue engine to pull it out and there it remains to this day. The hole was filled in and the engine languishes at the bottom. Christopher Awdry, the author's son, confirmed the authenticity of this link.

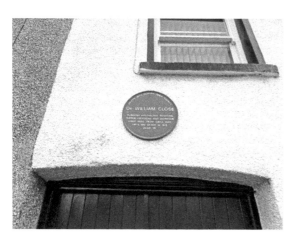

Blue plaque for Dr William Close.

The links to Barrow are strengthened even further by Revd Awdry's early maps of his fictional location, Sodor. The Bishops of the Isles were termed 'Bishops of Sodor and Man' and the fictional Sodor was located somewhere in the Irish Sea between Walney and the Isle of Man. This was confirmed by the addition of Barrow, Millom, Ulverston and Walney to the maps and Vickerstown became Vicarstown. This link continues with the suggestion that Sir James Ramsden was in fact the 'Fat Controller' of story fame; a little insulting, but one can see the resemblance in pictures of the two. Christopher Awdry, who continued his father's stories until 1992, wrote a book about the series and made many other connections which showed the influence Barrow & Furness Railway had on the authors. Some of the Furness Railway engines were used as subjects for the stories and later on the diesel engines that worked in the Furness area. Additionally, Awdry referred to Ravenglass & Eskdale Railway as well; although these aren't Barrow, the close links via the Furness Railway are evident.

Local history became a subject of great interest during the Victorian and Edwardian period. Barrow and Furness had been mentioned in numerous old texts, but this was the heyday of scholarly research. A number of writers and historians chose to write about the area in some detail and one of those wrote a definitive history of Furness Abbey. The man in question is Father Thomas West, a Jesuit priest. He resided at Tytup Hall, an attractive manor house on the outskirts of Dalton and Marton. It is built on the site of earlier buildings and presents an impressive frontage. The current building dates to the early eighteenth century and probably replaced an earlier house, possibly Orgrave Hall. This building was given by Sir Thomas Preston for the use of the Jesuits, who himself became a Jesuit and left the area for the Continent.

Father West wrote *The Antiquities of Furness* in 1774, a comprehensive history of Furness, in particular Furness Abbey. This was a major source for other later works and it is still a seminal history. It was a forerunner to West's *Guide to the Lakes*, which was published in 1778 and frequently reprinted. West was sent on a mission by the order to Furness in 1770. He was well respected but the mission was removed to Ulverston in 1779, the same year that West died at Sizergh. Tytup was sold and now it is a private dwelling. Roman Catholicism had been suppressed in the area and according to the records of the bishops of Chester there were only twenty-three papists in the area by 1767. This is reflected by the lack of churches in the area until the Victorian era, when, due to an influx of Irish workers, St Mary's Church was built in Barrow to accommodate them.

Others followed West's academic efforts and his work was used as a source for many of the later works. *Annales Furnesienses* was written in 1844 by Thomas Alcock Beck. Beck was from Hawkshead and he attended the grammar school, the same establishment in which Wordsworth had studied. He left Trinity College, Cambridge, in 1814 but did not take his degree. Beck was afflicted with a spinal condition for most of his life and he designed paths and access suitable for his invalid chair in his grounds at Esthwaite Lodge. He was an avid antiquarian and writer and he edited the *Itinerary of Furness* by Dr William Close. His history of the abbey was dedicated to Queen Victoria and was an important piece of work. Its engravings are spectacular and show us what the abbey looked like in the eighteenth century.

Dr William Close was a resident of Dalton for the latter part of his life. He had been born at Field Broughton in 1775 but spent his childhood living on Walney Island. Close became

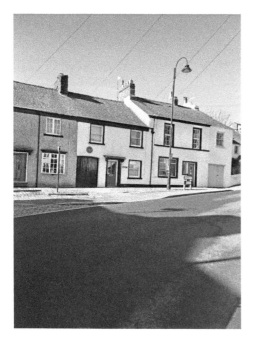

No. 2 Castle Street, Dalton.

an apprentice surgeon in Kendal in 1790 and he attended University of Edinburgh. He gained his medical diploma in 1797 and began practising in Dalton. He was a dedicated scholar – his interests including history, archaeology, art, music and writing. His acuity allowed him to develop other interests in engineering; he is credited with creating an engine that pumped water from mines. As a physician he was an early advocate of vaccination, and only three years after Dr Edward Jenner's pioneering cowpox vaccine was introduced, he inoculated poor children at his own cost and, assisted by the remote geography of the area, his actions removed the threat of smallpox in Furness.

He edited Beck's *Annales Furnesienses* and added notes as a supplement to the work. Close and Beck worked together at Close's cottage at No. 2 Castle Street, where there is a blue plaque commemorating him. Beck, in turn, edited the uncompleted work *Itinerary of Furness*, which Close was unable to finish due to illness. He died at the young age of thirty-six from tuberculosis in 1813, having achieved more in those brief years than many of us do in a lifetime.

DID YOU KNOW?

Footballer Emlyn Hughes, also known as 'Crazy Horse', was born in Barrow. He captained Liverpool and England throughout the 1970s. Latterly, he became a popular sport pundit on television and he was awarded an OBE. He is remembered in the National Football Museum Hall of Fame. His statue was unveiled in Abbey Road, Barrow, in 2008.

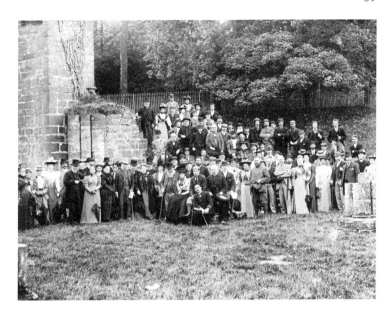

CWAAS visit to
Furness Abbey.
(Harper Gaythorpe
Collection)

Close can't be mentioned without reference to a successor of his, not only with reference to local history, but also as subsequent resident of No. 2 Castle Street, Dalton. Alice Leach was a teacher and keen local historian, who specialised in the history of Furness Abbey in particular. She was a founding member of the Barrow Civic and History Society and an authority on many subjects. She is well known for the many books she wrote about Furness Abbey and the town's history, and worked hard to capture the heritage of the area for future generations. She sadly died in 2014 and will be missed by many, but remembered by all.

The Cumberland, Westmorland Antiquarian and Archaeological Society celebrated its 150th anniversary in 2016 and the work they have done over those years is nothing short of remarkable. One notable member was Harper Gaythorpe, born in Tarporley, Cheshire, in 1850. He had an engraving business based in Harrison Street in Barrow and he soon became interested in his adopted town. He was a founding member of the Barrow Field Naturalists, becoming president in 1976. He was an indefatigable historian, writer and amateur archaeologist. He wrote reports and papers on many of the exciting archaeological finds in Furness, including the Rampside sword. He left behind many notebooks, drawings and photographs that form the Harper Gaythorpe Collection held at Cumbria Archives in Barrow Library. He lived at 'Claverton' (now Prospect House) on Prospect Road, later becoming an annexe to the Risedale Maternity Home. He wrote a biography of Dr William Close, lamenting that he was so little remembered beyond the Furness Peninsula. His keen interests included Furness Abbey, St Mary's Church, Walney, and Rampside. Gaythorpe died suddenly in 1909 but his work stands as testament to his dedication and focus.

A close friend of Gaythorpe was William Barrow Kendall, a true born 'Barrovian' born at Salthouse Farm in 1851. He was educated at Town Bank Grammar School, Ulverston. In 1867 he trained as a civil engineer for Furness Railway and qualified as AMICE. In the

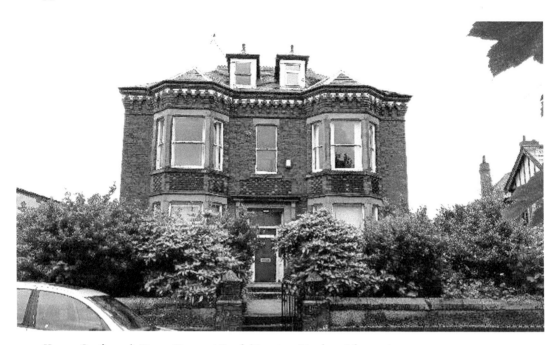

Harper Gaythorpe's House, Prospect Road. (Courtesy Matthew Johnston)

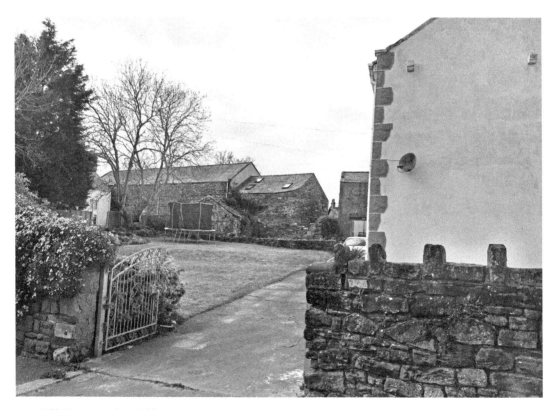

Old Farm complex, Salthouse.

early years he came into contact with the young engineer, James Ramsden, who lodged with Kendall for some years at Salthouse, the two becoming friends. It is tempting to imagine conversations between these two about the illustrious history of Barrow and the even more illustrious, hoped for future.

His first history project was the collection of information for a history of Salthouse. This possibly sparked his life-long love of history and antiquarian interests. He was a member of Barrow Naturalists' Field Club and was responsible for a number of important studies. Much of his work helped to give a fuller picture of the pre-industrial Barrow. He produced 'Glacial Deposits in Furness and District'; 'Submerged Peat Mosses, Forest Remains, and Post Glacial Deposits in Barrow Harbour' on 26 November 1880. 'The Conventual Buildings of Furness Abbey' followed on 26 May 1882.

DID YOU KNOW?

According to the Coucher Books (written at Furness to record its business and history) a 'felonious murder' was committed against Abbot Lawrence by three of his own monks in the thirteenth century. They plotted to kill him to gain his power and poisoned both his food and the sacramental chalice at Mass. He fell ill during the mass, bloating and becoming disorientated. He rushed to his chamber after Mass and eventually expired. Suspicions were aroused and caused a hue and cry, but the three monks took flight never to be seen again.

He moved to Harlesden in London in 1895 working for Mr Frank Stileman. He was able to continue his research and even extend it by constant visits to the Public Records Office. This work included 'Cocken: The History of a Furness Village' (delivered to the BNFC. on 16 November 1896) was the first result, followed by 'Northscale' (21 March 1898), 'Gleaston Castle' (on the site, 23 August 1902), 'Notes on the Village of Barrow' (6 January 1903), 'Waste of Coast Line, Furness and Walney in 1000 Years' (at Biggar, 23 July 1904) and 'Muchland and its Owners' (20 January 1908 and 24 December 1908). These were read by Mr Harper Gaythorpe and Kendall continued his association with Gaythorpe until his death in 1909.

Kendall himself died in 1919. Many papers were found after his death and later published. Much of the material was used by Paul V. Kelly in subsequent papers for the CWAAS. His work is still referred to today and provides an insight into early Barrow history.

6. Conflict, Religion and War

Between 1642 and 1660 the country was in conflict. Charles I had imposed heavy taxes and exerted his ideals of the divine right of kings by trying to dissolve Parliament. This brought him into direct dispute with the Commons and led to the English Civil War. Skirmishes and battles took place everywhere and the Furness Peninsula was no exception.

The Royalist army was led by Colonel Sir William Huddleston of Millom Castle, who rallied at Kirkby where there were a few supporters. They intended to move on Dalton and captured a number of Parliamentarian supporters. These prisoners were held at Dalton Castle, however those who escaped warned Colonel Rigby at Kirkby Lonsdale. He deployed troops to combat this Royalist threat and reached Ulverston on 30 September 1643. This force marched on Dalton the following day.

The Royalist troops were waiting at Lindal Close, barring the road to Dalton. There appears to have been a standoff initially, with the opposing troops hurling insults and shouting at one another. Rigby's smaller army, however, were carrying firearms and once the first shot was fired the Royalists started to retreat. The battle was over in a quarter of an hour, Huddleston was captured and his troops scattered or taken prisoner. Many were drowned on their way back over the sands to Millom and 400 were taken prisoner. The will to fight for the king's cause seemed less than enthusiastic and they were less well equipped or trained than their Parliamentarian counterparts. Dalton was plundered and ransacked following the decisive rout and marked the only significant encounter with the opposing sides.

However, the Royalist cause was still important in some quarters. The remnants of Prince Rupert's army, under Sir John Maney, were tasked with collecting rents due to the Crown, to fund the conflict further. This small force included a small regiment led by Sir John Preston of Furness Abbey. The Royalists marched to North Scale, a village on Walney Island in 1644. This was the site of the final hostilities in Furness during the Civil War. The village was besieged by Parliamentarian forces from the fleet harboured at Piel. The Royalists were beaten back by the Parliamentarians on the first attempt, which was particularly difficult considering the tidal nature of the island. When they finally attacked again the village was deserted. This incensed the Royalist troops, who exacted revenge by burning the houses to the ground, leaving only the two known Royalist homes standing, one of which still survives.

Occasionally, Barrow has slipped into the national historical record. One such occasion was when George Fox, the founder of Quakerism, came to the district. His time in Furness was marred by conflict and opposition to his ideas. In 1652 Fox arrived in North Scale to speak to the curate. He was unsuccessful in locating him and ended up visiting James Lancaster. It appears that Lancaster was interested in the ideas that Fox presented and converted to the ideals.

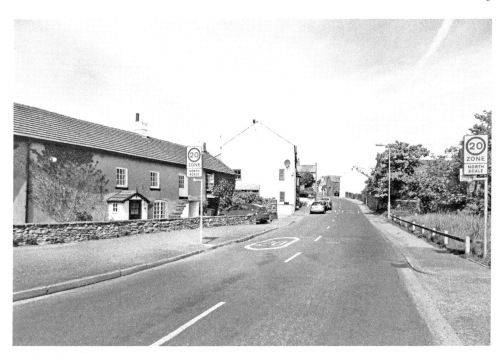

North Scale village.

Fox was heartened by this minor success and decided he would return to see if more of the village would be convinced. This time he was not met with friendship but with blows. He was prevented from entering the village and was rendered unconscious by the sticks and cudgels of the villagers. When he came to, he was met with James Lancaster's wife throwing stones at him; evidently she was not as 'convinced' as her husband. Indeed it appears she had been persuaded by the villagers that Fox had bewitched her husband. Lancaster intervened and probably saved Fox from more serious injury. He managed to push the boat offshore with the injured Fox still in it, in order for him to escape to the mainland. Fox, not surprisingly, never returned to Walney. One interesting and odd fact is that both of the Lancasters did become Quakers and James actually joined Fox on Gospel missions and went to the Americas with him. Fox had been unfortunate in Ulverston too, being beaten for his beliefs in the 'Steeple House', and as he reports in his journal,

> they fell upon me in the Steeple-house before his Face, and knock't me down, and kickt me, and trampled upon me, he looking on; And so great was the Uproar, that some People tumbled over their Seats for fear.

As noted earlier Barrow did not have a Roman Catholic church for worshippers and Fisher mentions in his diary the death of a child of six months who was buried at Walney 'without any serimony being of the Romen perswason'. This absence of Roman Catholic churches would be rectified as people flooded into the area from other places such as

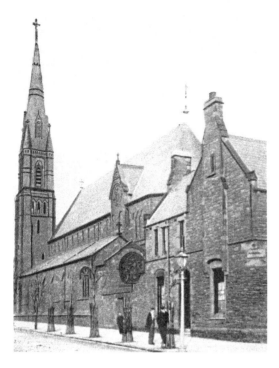

St Mary's RC Church, Barrow.

Ireland. Many had sought work in Barrow after the exodus from the potato famine in 1845, a gradual stream of Irish families came from their initial destination in Liverpool. The conditions they lived in were poor and wages were inequitable. In the mid-nineteenth century this led to wage riots, which finally drew attention to the inequality. Many lived on Barrow Island and Hindpool and eventually they were given their own St Mary's Church in Duke Street, with others like St Patrick's springing up later as the population grew.

Second World War

Naturally Barrow-in-Furness was a target for the Luftwaffe in Second World War. The steelworks and the shipyard were heavily involved in the war effort. Mini submarines, ships and armaments were in rapid production during the war and they were always on alert for air-raid attacks.

In 1936 the *Hindenburg* flew over the town. The huge German zeppelin was an elite form of transport for the rich and they were on the return journey from the United States of America. It was not by chance that the craft flew low over the town; witnesses on the ground could clearly see the Nazi swastikas emblazoned on its tail fins. It caused a great stir in the town and was reported by the local press. This trip gave the Nazis an opportunity to extensively photograph the town, in particular the shipyard, from the air. This was obviously in preparation for future conflict and gave them very accurate pictures that would assist them in map making and would be used by the Luftwaffe during bombing raids.

DID YOU KNOW?

William Forshaw VC was born in 1890 in Barrow-in-Furness. He was in action in Gallipoli, Turkey, and held the north-west corner of 'The Vineyard' against heavy attacks from the Turkish army. He was awarded the highest honour given in battle for bravery – the Victoria Cross. He died in 1943 in Berkshire and his campaign medals are displayed in the Museum of Manchester Regiment.

Air-raid precautions were begun in 1939, ranging from the gas mask distribution centres, and provision of masks, to the installation of basic air-raid precautions and shelters. As the shipyard was an obvious target, the town began to prepare. Public shelters were created in a number of places but were inadequate for the needs of the town. There are stories of people leaving during bombing raids to the countryside to escape the danger. Many of the central areas around the town were hit, with a high loss of life. In April 1941 a number of building were destroyed and people injured or killed, including the vicar and verger of the church in Abbey Road, now commemorated by Coronation Gardens. There was a direct hit of the hammer head crane in Vickers Shipyard in May of that year and two fire watchers were killed. Many people who lost their homes in surrounding streets were forced to evacuate, many to family and friends in the countryside where it was deemed to be safer – for example in Askam, Ireleth and Kirby.

DID YOU KNOW?

The *Sky News* presenter Stephen Dixon was born in Newton-in-Furness in 1974. He presents the morning news programme 'Sunrise' and he was the first newsreader to report on the London bombings in 2005.

Many of the defences are easily spotted even today, their concrete construction hardly altering in the intervening years. Pillboxes and gun emplacements were placed around the docks and Walney. The pillboxes were built from reinforced concrete to provide maximum protection and were an integral part of the country's defences. These guard posts were equipped with loopholes to allow those inside to use firearms, while being protected from small arms fire and grenades. They were often raised to allow for better visibility and a clear field of fire. The design of the eight-sided pillbox was created during the First World War and were originally part of the trench system.

Those along the Barrow coastline and docks were strategically placed to alert the town if an invasion appeared from the Irish Sea. One really well preserved example, which really is hidden from view, is located at the junction of Roose and Rampside Roads. It stands on the small hill above the road, again strategically placed; now surrounded by bushes, but it

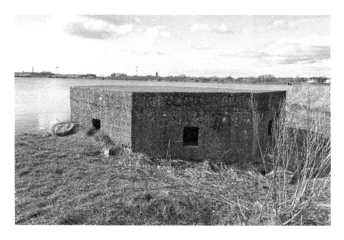

Pillbox, Cavendish Dock.

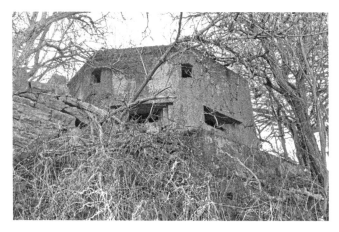

Pillbox, Roose.

would have been quite prominent when first built. Thankfully they were never tested as a defence mechanism by invasion, but were probably useful for observation and the sight of them would raise the confidence of the population when seeing this obvious symbol of defence.

DID YOU KNOW?

Barrow-born journalist Philip Geddes, aged twenty-four, was killed in the IRA bomb at Harrods, Knightsbridge, on 17 December 1983. Geddes was responding to the news of a telephone bomb warning. He was caught in the blast at 1.30 p.m. and sadly died. There is a memorial at the site of the blast and annual prizes in honour of Mr Geddes are awarded to young journalism students at University of Oxford. A Philip Geddes Memorial Lecture is held annually, delivered by a leading journalist, a poignant reminder that simple journalism can sometimes place the reporter in harm's way.

Anti-aircraft headquarters was located at the Furness Abbey Hotel, beside Furness Abbey and railway station. The hotel was a popular tourist venue in its heyday and was closely linked to the adjoining station and ticket office. It was shielded by the trees in the valley and Abbotswood but this did not protect it. In May 1941 it was seriously bombed and damaged, and in the same month Barrow Central Station was also hit and badly damaged. The hotel was demolished after the war, but the second class buffet and ticket office became the Abbey Tavern, which is now in the hands of English Heritage.

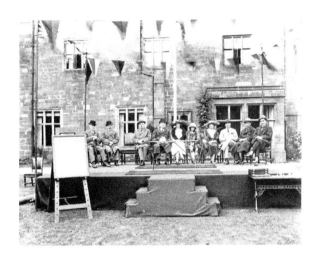

Iron and Steel Works Presentation,
Furness Abbey Hotel, 1919.

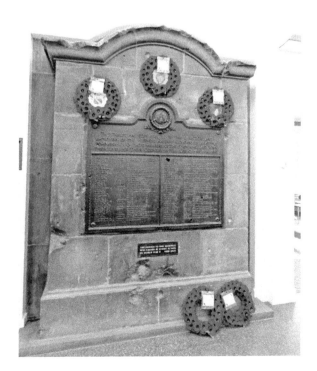

Furness Railway memorial,
Barrow Station.

The only tangible sign of bomb damage to the Central Station is shrapnel damage to the memorial of the Furness Railway dead of the First World War. Sixty-eight names are recorded on the memorial but 515 employees of Furness Railway signed up for military service. The memorial was unveiled by the 9th Duke of Devonshire, Victor Christian William Cavendish, on the 16 October 1921 and dedicated by F. J. Ramsden. The author's great uncle, William Cowan, 1st Battalion Border Regiment, is one of the fallen named,

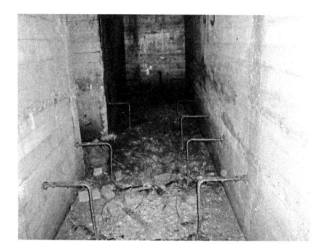

Left: Underground air-raid shelter, Barrow Island. (Courtesy of K. Millard)

Below: Plan of underground shelters. (Courtesy of K. Millard)

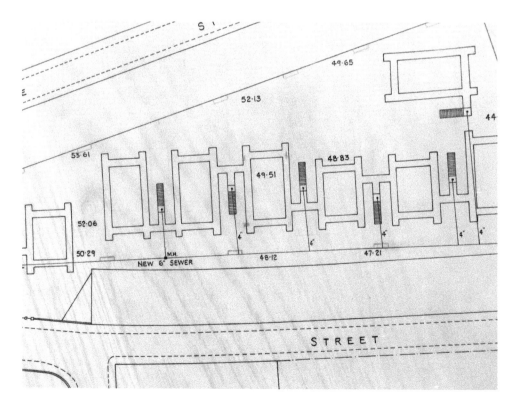

falling at Arras in 1917 aged twenty-four. The bomb damage is still visible, both on the sandstone and in the metal plaque, which is an ironic reminder that the hope that the First World War was the war to end all wars was not to be.

Public shelters were provided but evidence of these is limited now. There were public shelters for example at Barrow Grammar School, in Duke Street and on Barrow Island. The shelters at Barrow Island have recently been rediscovered during routine building work. The extent of them is quite staggering and the warren of tunnels provides a virtual time capsule of this dangerous period. Barrow Island would have been a sitting target, the shipyard being located within it. The shelters were necessary to provide some protection for the local population. The shelters here are fascinating, having graffiti and artefacts left behind as though the inhabitants had vacated yesterday. The poignant drawing of Mickey Mouse brings the realisation that it must have been terrifying for young children – maybe the picture was drawn by a mum or dad trying to distract their offspring? The tunnels are sealed up and have disappeared from view now, which seems a shame. I am sure it would be an interesting heritage venue but the environment would possibly not meet the rigour of current health and safety demands.

A little-known piece of wartime history is found beneath the bridge on The Strand. The entrance is set back and hardly noticeable, but it is here that The Strand 'British Restaurant' was located. It was part of the response by the Ministry of Food in the Second World War to help to supply food for those who needed it during the conflict. People

Left: Entrance to air-raid shelters.

Right: Mickey Mouse graffiti.

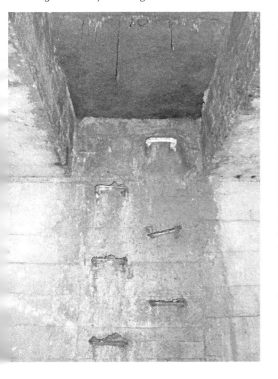
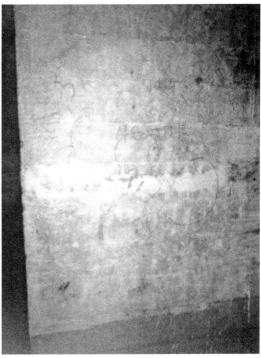

were displaced and were sometimes challenged by the strictures of the war to provide themselves and families with wholesome meals. It was essential to have a healthy community to assist in the war effort and this was one way of ensuring this. The initiative was countrywide and nourishing food was produced at a reasonable price for those who needed it. The location of the restaurant is quite protected beneath the Michaelson Road Bridge and was a reinforced structure within an existing building. This would also possibly provide some protection as an air-raid shelter. There was another 'Community Feeding Centre' at the old Public Hall. This building no longer exists, but was behind the Town Hall where the car park is now. These establishments existed into the 1950s when rationing was still operating.

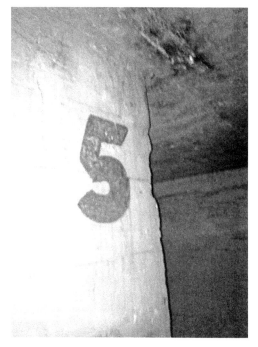

Shelter number 5.

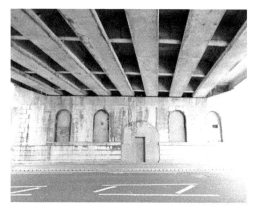

British restaurant The Strand.

7. Hidden from View

Barrow-in-Furness was never traditionally the civic and administrative centre for the area. Dalton-in-Furness, 4 miles from the town, claims its prominence as the 'ancient capital'. This is essentially true, being established by the monks as the judicial and administrative centre and gaining a market charter in 1239. However, following the Industrial Revolution it was overtaken by the newly burgeoning town of Barrow. Even today there is gentle rivalry between its residents, but Barrow soon outstripped it as an urban conurbation. The difference between the two settlements is obvious. Dalton is an organic town that grew around the church and castle and is centred around the main route to Barrow and the coast and in the other direction to Ulverston. Barrow, in contrast, is mostly planned and linear; the old routes have been absorbed and widened but can be identified as ancient trackways by comparing on old maps.

Sometimes the only environmental clues to the purpose and appearance of locations are in the names that still remain. One such clue is in the real name for St George's Hill. This was better known as Rabbit Hill and refers to an earlier time when there was an abbey warren there for the use of the monks. This name was passed down and remained in common usage until the late nineteenth century, when the town fathers altered the name to the grander sounding St George's Hill, reflecting its later incarnation and civic importance.

Abbey Road was the main route from Dalton to Barrow. Previously referred to as Barrow Lane, it emerged from Market Street in Dalton by passing Furness Abbey and continuing to the town. This traditional route was widened and made into an impressive tree-lined avenue, finally arriving at Ramsden Square. It once continued into what is

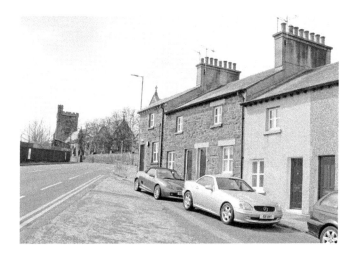

Rabbit Hill, St George's Hill.

now known as Dalton Road, which went up the hill and connected with the original village. Another ancient trackway was Greengate, again a widened road over a traditional route – this time to Roose Mill. It was a rural road and roughly follows the old medieval route. Friars Lane, which bisects the old route, was known as Salthouse Lane, which, as previously mentioned, would have been a route from the salt pans to Furness Abbey.

DID YOU KNOW?

Dame Stella Rimington, who was brought up in Barrow, became the first female Director General of MI5 in 1992 and the first publicly acknowledged DG the following year.

The Pinfold in Dalton is a small enclosure built from local limestone dating to the eighteenth century. It is set back from Abbey Road at Goose Green, just below the church at Dalton. This was created to contain any stray animals such as sheep, horses or cows that appeared in the village. They were captured and placed there until their owners came to retrieve them. They would have to pay a small fine to the 'pinder' to release them. Pinders were employed by the local leading townsmen and the name has passed down to families in the district.

Goose Green is an interesting place with a wealth of hidden heritage. Local tradition has it that the green was used as an assembly point for the town's bowmen before they went to the archery butts (at Butts Beck) to practise their archery. This was a legal requirement for boys and men to ensure that a source of archers were always ready to provide service to the lord of the manor.

This was also the site of the first free school in Dalton, founded by Thomas Boulton, who bequeathed a sum of money in 1622 to be used to run it. It was built at the foot of the

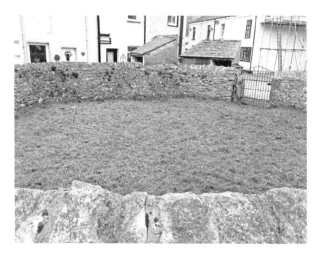

Pinfold, Dalton.

cliff near to the vicarage and there is a plaque to commemorate this bequest in the parish church. Much later a boys' national school was opened in 1862 and later a girls' school in 1878. The Victorian building, known as the Greens School, remains but is now a popular venue for weddings and food and is known as 'Chequers'. Set back from the Pinfold is a row of old cottages. These look innocuous enough but were once a place to be feared and avoided. This was the Dalton Workhouse, opened in 1826 and replacing the previous poorhouse at Billincoat. Rules were harsh and life inside was even harder; it would have a last resort for anyone to enter these premises. A terrible testament of this is the story of a destitute and pregnant girl in labour, who was ejected from the workhouse because she was a resident of Cumberland. The Parish Board did not want the expense of looking after her and the child and she was removed and driven away in a cart. This caused damage and the poor girl died before delivery of the baby was complete. The case was brought as in inquiry but it appears the worst punishment meted out was a fine.

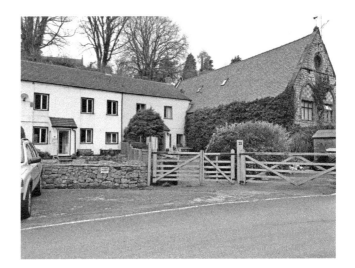

Old Dalton Workhouse.

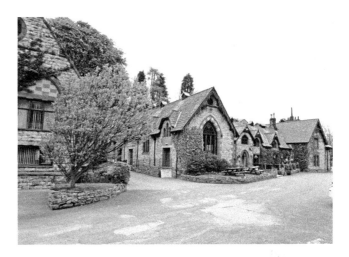

Greens School, Dalton.

Another hidden piece of history is located across the road beneath a car saleroom and garage. There is now no trace of the gasworks that provided the town with gas until 1948. This was built on land belonging to the Furness Railway and was once again part of the industrial planning of the area.

The Billings

The name is taken from the Old English word 'Bilk' or sword edge. This was probably used as a description of the shape of the hill. It is a prominent hill and is easily visible from the main routes into Barrow. It was chosen as the location for planting trees to represent the Prince of Wales' feathers in order to commemorate his visit to Barrow. This project was not completed, but if one looks carefully towards the Billings one side of the curve of the feather is visible still.

Blind Lane

Part of the public highway, which would probably be an ancient trackway, was closed in 1857. Blind Lane led from Mill Brow to the village of Newton and had been in use for centuries. It was closed to preserve the privacy of Sir James Ramsden and his family, who lived at the newly built Abbotswood. It became a private carriageway and was also used

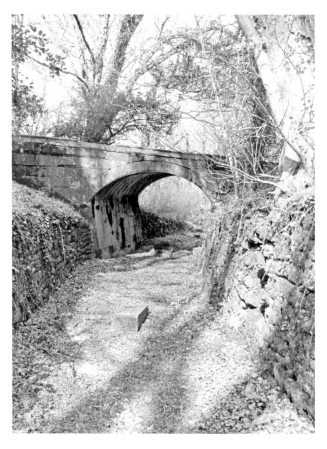

Blind Lane, under driveway.

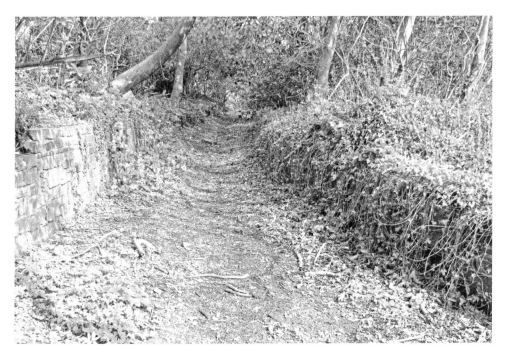

Blind Lane.

by servants to reach the house. A path veered towards the mansion so that the servants would not be visible as they approached. The road can be traced through Abbotswood and emerged approximately where the lane to Dalton is now. A small pathway is an indicator of the final part of the route over the fields to Newton.

Crivelton

Crivelton or Clivertun is another lost village in the Furness area. It fell from use well before the disappearance of Sellergarth. The vill is mentioned in the Domesday Book and although a rough location is suggested, once again there is no material evidence to confirm this. It is listed after Lies (Leece), Glassertun (Gleaston) and Steintun (Stainton). These villages still exist and they are inland. It seems possible that Criveltun lay somewhere towards the coast, past Rosse (Roose) and towards Rampside. Barnes (1968) alleges that the Crivelton of the monks was most likely renamed Newtown and lies between Page Bank and Peasholmes. Why this settlement fell out of use is not known and is one of the places only remembered in field names and dusty documents.

It might make sense for its location to be in this vicinity considering the long establishment of a church at Rampside. The church is unusual in that there is no settlement close by. This has lately become an issue as the congregation tend to use a building in the village a mile away along the coast rather than at this outpost; the church is now under threat of closure. Presumably, at some earlier time there might have been a small hamlet or village closer to it. It has been suggested that the church is the last in a succession of churches and it is mentioned by the monks as early as 1292. There is evidence to suggest

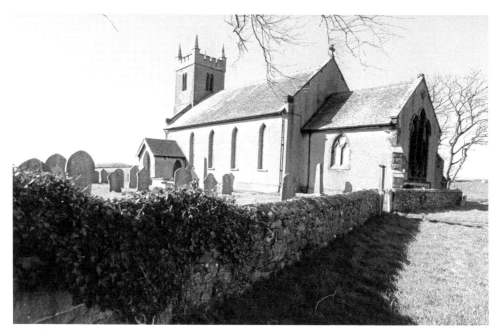

St Michael's Church, Rampside.

it might have been the site of an earlier place of worship and it appears to be built upon a mound of some kind. The present church was rebuilt in 1840, but the earlier building dated to 1621. It was one of the chapels in Furness that George Fox, the Quaker, preached from after the Sunday service. He was successful in converting the minister and botanist Thomas Lawson, who became a Quaker and writer of religious works.

DID YOU KNOW?
Dave Myers, the Hairy Biker, was born and raised in Barrow. He attended the local boys' grammar school and later attended Goldsmith's University of London. Until recently the television chef lived in his hometown too and is one of its strongest advocates.

Salthouse and Sandgate

Salt was an important commodity in medieval times. It was the one reliable way to preserve food for the winter and keep it edible. The monks had to ensure they had a ready supply and fortunately the location of Furness Abbey was not too far from the sea. The Sandgate was until recently remembered in the name of the public house at the entrance to Cavendish Docks. The Sandgate was where the monks would have access to the sands and marshes that were covered by the sea at high tide. This left a residue of salt for them

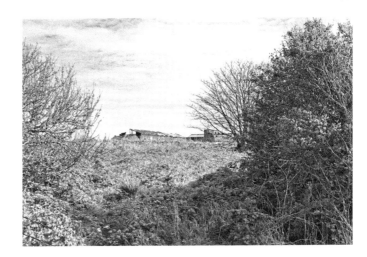

Salthouse Mills.

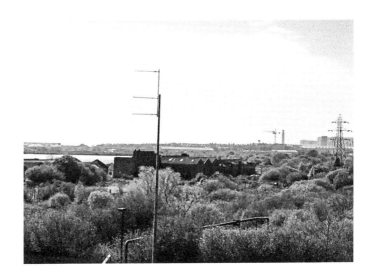

Salthouse Mills and
Cavendish Dock.

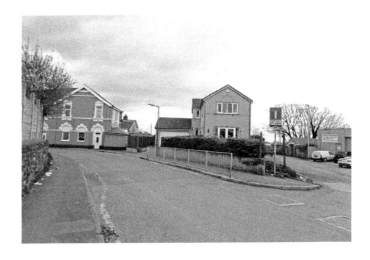

The Sandgate.

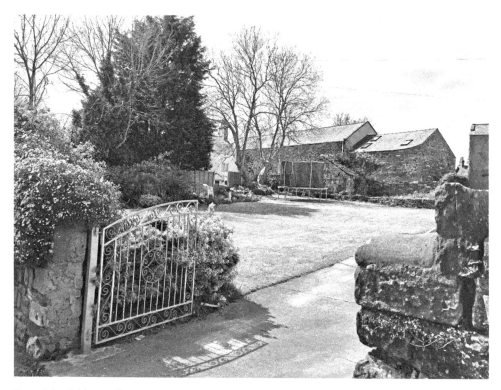

One of the Salthouse farms.

to extract. A large reservoir would have been dug out to hold the sea water from high tides; this water would evaporate during periods of low tide and the salt residue drained into a lower covered basin. Here it would be cleaned and then removed to the boiling pans in the Salt House where the water would be evaporated, leaving only the salt. This would then be packed and removed to the abbey.

A salt house was built at this location to process the salt and this is again remembered in the name of the roads Salthouse Road and Marsh Street. The salt marshes stretched to where the derelict Salthouse Mills now stands and some of the land is returning to grassland. This area is expected to be redeveloped soon, a grand marina and housing plan has been produced for the council and it aims to renovate this sadly derelict area. The routes to the abbey that would have been used to take the salt are still evident. These radiate from the abbey to the coast connecting granges along the way.

Abbotswood

The mansion built for Sir James Ramsden, the managing director of Furness Railway and the first mayor of the newly incorporated borough of Barrow-in-Furness, was a grand country house designed by E. G. Paley. It was a showpiece for the company and it was intended to provide Ramsden with the appropriate status and give him a place to entertain clients of the companies he managed. After his death it passed to his son Frederic, who never married. It fell into disrepair after Frederic died in 1941 and was used by the army as a camp facility. In the 1960s the house had deteriorated so much that the local Barrow Corporation decided to demolish it. Evidently their estimate of its deterioration was inaccurate, because to destroy it the council had to use dynamite. Following this, a civil defence bunker was built and this too passed into history – no trace is left today. The wood is now a popular nature reserve and walk but although many people use it they are often unaware of the history beneath their feet and around them, hidden in plain sight.

At the location of the house, there are huge sandstone blocks marking the site. It overlooks a sharp drop into the wood below and stands above the railway line and the abbey. At the foot of this ravine is a great deal of demolition rubble, forgotten and overgrown. There are tiles, bricks and other interesting fragments to be found and it is remarkable that these are still here. In the gardens above hints of the original building are scattered around and a keen eye can soon spot them. The sandstone pillars of the gateway at the back of the site are a reminder of the grand driveway from Mill Brow, which would have brought visitors to the mansion. The drive has disappeared beneath the field, but its footprint can be seen in certain light conditions. There is evidence of an ornate garden, with walks and pathways. Some of the structures still remain, including an attractive sandstone gateway and steps, almost hidden in the bushes in front of the site of the house. Further back to the right of the site is the location of the orchard and the greenhouses. When looking at old photographs of these it is not hard to imagine how

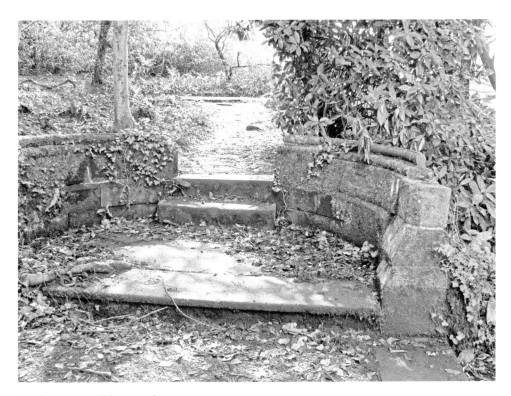

Garden steps at Abbotswood.

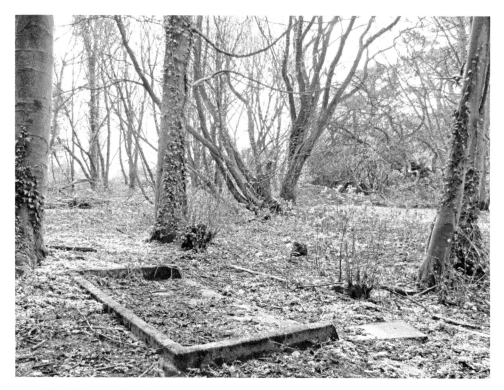

Second World War archaeology, Abbotswood.

magnificent the grounds would have been. Small reminders appear in the woods and the grass, such as the metal arches and posts that still remain defiantly visible. Again looking very carefully, pot shards and pieces of glass can be found in the undergrowth.

Even deeper into the wood, suddenly new discoveries are made. The remains of toilet blocks from the army camp in the 1940s erupt through the undergrowth, incongruous in this country setting. It seems astonishing that the demolition was not as complete as it might have been and the sight of this takes the visitor by surprise.

Of course Abbotswood stretches back further into history and there is evidence of this too, but again it is easily overlooked. The assumption is that the woodland stretched around the abbey on all sides of the valley and this is where the monks found their supply of wood. The current wood is contained in Victorian boundaries, but within this the ancient perimeter wall is visible. There is a particularly well-preserved section that cuts into the wood near the driveway. It is almost the full height it was originally, around 3 metres, and it is conserved by English Heritage.

Such an impressive house could not completely disappear; the remnants are still visible in the grounds and the gatehouses are also still visible and are inhabited. The private railway siding, which was created for Ramsden to board and alight the train, is no longer there but it is easy to spot where it was. The only trace of the railway station is the Abbey Tavern, now under the care of English Heritage. This was the second class buffet and ticket office, which later became a popular pub and bistro until it was abandoned

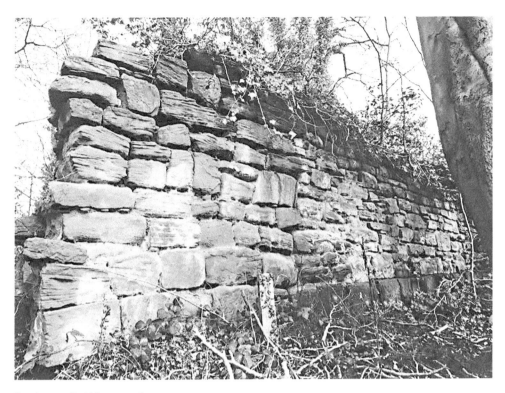

Precinct wall, Abbotswood.

in 2009. The outer fabric of the building is quite impressive, with carved gargoyles and a Gothic style. On the rear wall fragments of original carved bricks from the first Savigniac monastery can be spotted.

DID YOU KNOW?

Peter Purves, the *Blue Peter* presenter and TV personality, lived in Barrow-in-Furness in his teens and attended the local sixth form. His parents had a newsagent on Oxford Street and Purves joined the local Barrow Repertory Co. He acted in *Doctor Who* and presented *Crufts* and has had a number of other cameo performances in various productions.

The history of Furness Abbey is irrevocably intertwined with Abbotswood and Ramsden. His intrusion into the valley was complete with the building of the mansion house in the woods above. The Gothic style of the house echoed the medieval abbey buildings and certain aspects of the decor were also embellished with remnants from the ruins. The contents of the mansion were redistributed after Frederic's death and much of it ended up in Barrow Town Hall – yet another Victorian Gothic masterpiece.

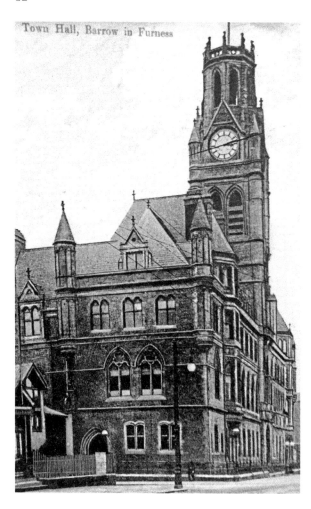

Barrow Town Hall.

Some of the stained glass from Abbotswood allegedly ended up adorning the windows in the Town Hall. These give a nod to the monastic history of the abbey in the pictures of the monks. There are also pieces of furniture in the upstairs gallery and the council chamber that purport to come from Abbotswood.

An oak relief carving of Pharoah and the Egyptians being drowned in the Red Sea is situated on the grand staircase wall and is apparently another artefact from Furness Abbey. Its provenance has not been confirmed but it is likely that interesting pieces, which remained in the abbey at the dissolution, would have been sold or passed on; the Preston family will surely have benefitted from these in the new manor house they built. When this structure was demolished and replaced by the Furness Abbey Hotel and station, those artefacts will probably have been reused in both the hotel and mansion. There are two marble reliefs that were rescued from the hotel at its demise – now in the care of English Heritage. One was until recently on display but has joined the other for conservation. These almost certainly did originate from the abbey and will hopefully return to be displayed at Furness Abbey.

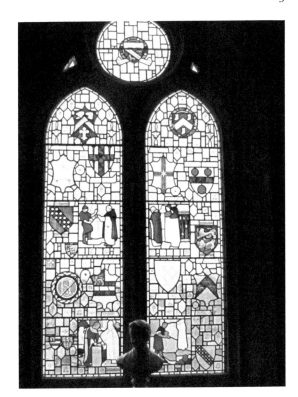

Right: Stained glass from Abbotswood.

Below: Wooden carved relief in Town Hall.

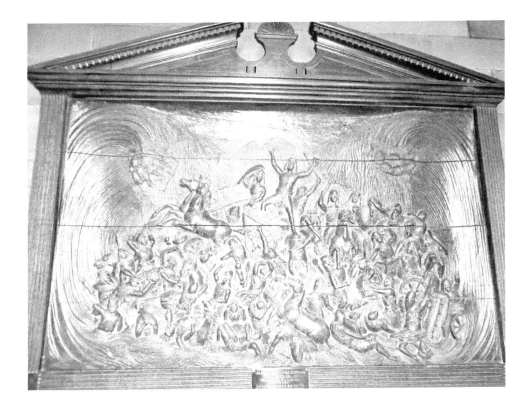

Michaelson House

Michaelson House was the family home of the Michaelson family who lived on Barrow Island, or 'Old Barrow' as it was known. They owned the island having inherited it through marriage since 1700. The island was not connected to the mainland and was rural in nature. The Michaelsons built a grand house in 1726 and this was further added to by following generations. The family were wealthy and there are records of their assets and costs; these included wages for five male servants, carriages, horses, including race horses, and even greyhounds.

Thomas Michaelson, who lived from 1814 to 1855 (buried in Walney churchyard), was married to Jane Gibson. Her family had previously owned the island before the Michaelsons inherited it. She was appointed guardian of the estate after her husband died. She was a talented landscape painter and painted the mansion, these showing how grand it must have been and how starkly different the view of the island is now. She was responsible for building a school on Walney Island for the people who lived there. In 1863 she sold the estate to the Duke of Devonshire and the Furness Railway, helping them to develop their plans for expansion and shipbuilding, totally transforming the island. The mansion was demolished during the First World War and there is no trace left.

The Michaelsons are mentioned in the diary of William Fisher (1811–59). One poignant entry in July 1843, 'at the Isle of Barrow the Lady of T.Y.P Michaelson of a son and air', followed a few days later with, 'Died at the Isle of Barrow the infant son of T.Y.P Michaelson Esq.' This is illustrative that infant mortality could affect any class.

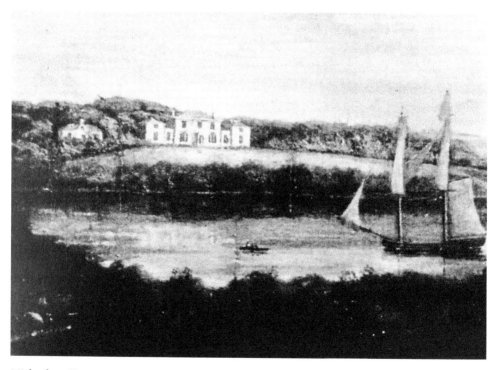

Michaelson House.

Roose village has changed over the last hundred years. The central hub of the village, with its sandstone terraced cottages and school, are still present, but the surroundings have been developed and changed. New houses have sprung up in the most unlikely places, eradicating some important historical markers. One of these is at the junction of North Row and Rampside Road. Originally, this was the location for St Perran's Mission Church, now demolished and the site covered by a bungalow and a new house, recently built. No trace remains of its original use, despite the church only becoming defunct in 2014. The last building was constructed in 1967 to replace the earlier Victorian tin hut, which served as church hall and Sunday school. Behind this was a small wooden church in which services were held. The old church hall burnt down in 1965 during a Christmas fair when the old stove chimney became separated because high winds lifted the roof.

The mission church was built to serve the local community of Cornish miners and this is why it was dedicated to St Perran (St Piran), who is the patron saint of Cornwall. It was one of the churches in the parish of St Georges. St Luke's Church, which was a larger and grander affair, was dedicated in 1964 on Roose Road, replacing an earlier church. This

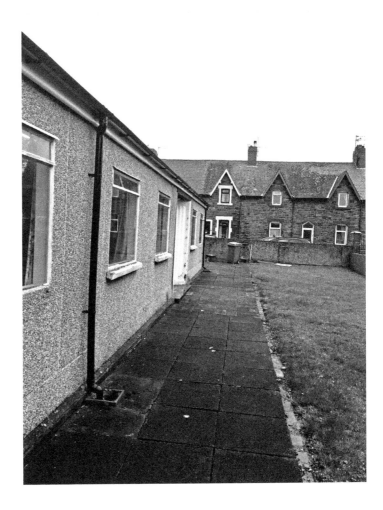

St Perran's Church, North Row.

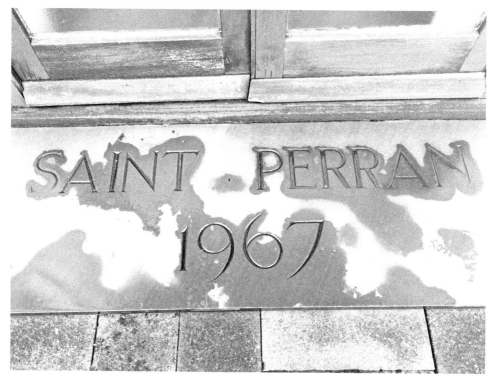

St Perran's date stone.

too has succumbed to smaller congregations and rising maintenance costs. It was sadly demolished in 2016, again with no trace left – it seems right to mention it here.

The Methodist chapel at Stonedyke has suffered a similar sad fate, as congregations dwindled the building was sold off. Latterly, the Methodist congregation shared St Perran's Church, but now that too has gone. The Methodist faith was very popular in Cornwall and naturally some of the miners would wish to worship in their own chapel. The chapel is now in a state of dereliction and is in private hands. It would be sad to see its neglect continue as it is an important building in the history of the Cornish miners.

Roose has extended in size to the west of the original village. The site on the hill where Roose Hospital once stood is now covered by a small housing estate. The hospital was originally a parish workhouse. Until 1876 Barrow had been part of the Ulverston Union, but as the town grew it was appropriate to provide relief for its own poor. Paupers from Barrow and parts of Dalton were to be accommodated in a temporary building in Dalkeith Street until the new workhouse was built at Roose.

The site was large and imposing and could be seen for miles around. It was large enough to house 300 inmates and was completed in 1878–79. It finally opened the following year covering almost 8 acres. The report in the *Barrow Herald* boasting that 'the view from the building is the best'; it would be interesting to know whether the inmates appreciated this view quite as much as the guardians. There were two wards, one for females and one

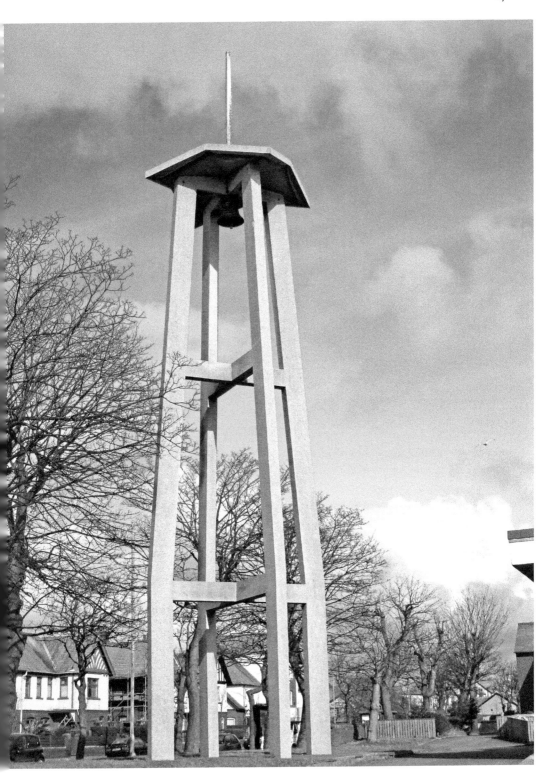

St Luke's bell tower.

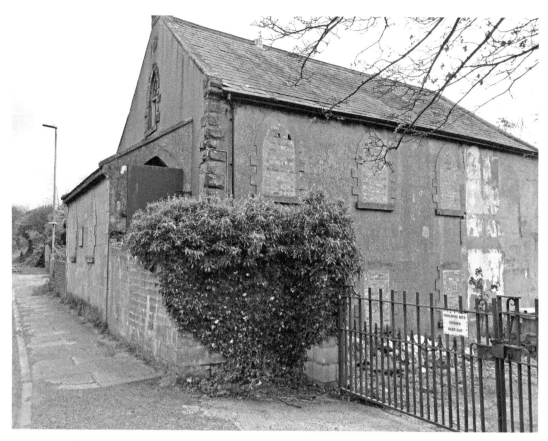

Stonedyke Methodist Chapel.

for males. Within these wards the inmates were grouped together according to age and ability in order to 'bring about the greatest possible discipline'.

The foundation stone was laid by Mrs H. W. Schneider on 12 September 1878, a civic event witnessed by the Parish Guardians of Barrow-in-Furness. Many of the usual dignitaries were included in this group – H. W. Schneider, Sir James Ramsden and Mr E. Wadham to name but a few. The great and the good saw it as their civic duty to provide for the needy but, of course, in the usual strict Victorian manner. Workhouse provision was not a free ride and conditions were harsh. It was a last resort for the paupers who were unfortunate enough to need it and it was designed to be so. The residents were expected to work for their keep: there was a yard for stone breaking, gardens for cultivating the necessary vegetables for use in the institution and other tasks to help with the smooth running of the place. Indeed this concept was again remarked upon by the *Barrow Herald*, that 'a satisfactory feature' of the new building was that 'all vagrants will have to earn the cost of their lodgings and food before they go on their way'. The workhouse changed its use in 1949 and became a hospital specialising in gynaecology and geriatric medicine. It still held connotations of fear for those who could recall its original use and it looked foreboding as it stood among the trees on the hill. From 1949

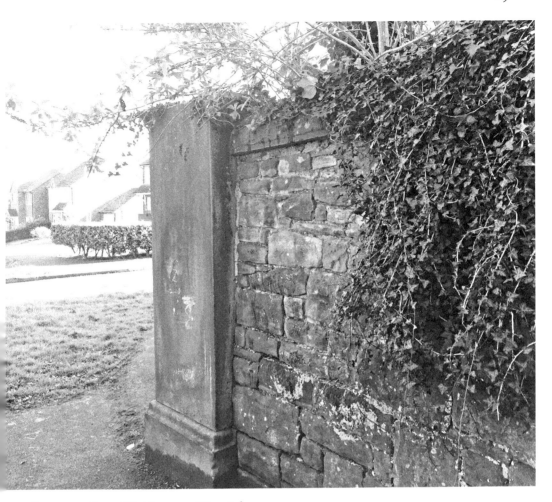

Entrance to Roose Workhouse and Hospital.

to the early 1980s it continued as a hospital until it was closed because the new Furness General Hospital was opened.

The old building became derelict and neglected and was demolished in the 1990s. On the site now is a small residential estate, pleasant and leafy, a far cry from the imposing presence of the workhouse. There are still hints in the landscaping of the previous incarnation of this area: the original wall, which bounded the grounds along the lane to Rampside Road, is in part still there. A solitary gate post, without the capstone, stands alone to declare the main entrance to the site. The street names Stoneham, Dowie, Liddle and Armon echo the past, named after doctors and gynaecologists who worked in the hospital – a slightly unusual idea possibly. The final street, Redshaw Avenue, is randomly named after Sir Leonard Redshaw, who was the deputy chairman of Vickers Shipyard – perhaps they ran out of gynaecologists.

Roa Island has many hints in the environment that can be easily overlooked. One such building is the impressive watchtower facing onto the channel and looking towards

Barrow and Walney. It was built in 1847 as a Customs and Excise House and certainly held a prime position. Traditionally Roa and Piel were integral to the monitoring of customs and excise – excise officers and pilots were based at Piel back to the seventeenth century. There were stories of smuggling even back to the monastic times – the monks were often chastised for avoiding excise duty. The position of the two locations is perfect for monitoring sea traffic along the Irish Sea. The watchtower is no longer used but stands against the sea observing all the sea traffic in and out of Barrow.

The connection with the sea is strong and along the front of the island facing Piel is a row of cottages built by Trinity House for the ten pilots who serviced the channel. They are simple terraced cottages but have withstood the weather for many years. Trinity Terrace is now privately owned and each cottage has its own style and charm.

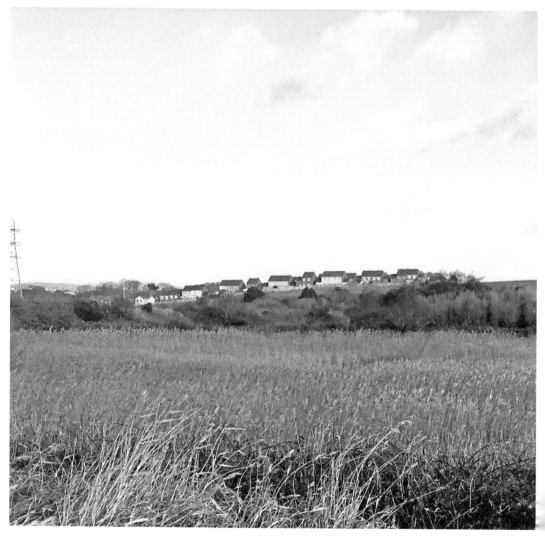

The site of Roose Hospital on the hill.

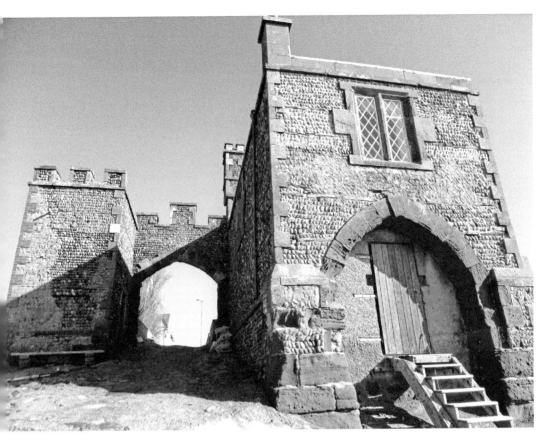

Watchtower, Roa Island.

The green, which was in front of them, has in recent years been fenced off to provide gardens for the cottages.

Another interesting item is the war memorial plaque at Roa Island. It is a retrospective memorial, placed there in 1993. It commemorates the gesture of the Duke of Buccleuch, who gave Piel Island to the people of Barrow in 1920 for the fallen in the First World War. It is unusual to have an island as a memorial and again it is a hidden piece of heritage. The current stone plaque was provided by Barrow Civic Society, Friends of Furness Abbey, Furness and Cartmel Tourism and the Rampside Women's Institute. It was unveiled in September 1993 by the then mayor of Barrow, Cllr Hazel Edwards.

The diary of William Fisher is an extremely interesting footnote to the early history of Barrow-in-Furness. Fisher was a local yeoman farmer at the very time that Barrow began its rapid transformation from rural village to industrial powerhouse. He was born in 1775 and died in 1861 and must have witnessed many changes. His diary covers the period from 1811 to 1859 and is really a record of events locally rather than a reflective piece. He catalogues the births, marriages and deaths of the people in his community, which is not just limited to the village; indeed he makes reference to people across Low Furness and beyond.

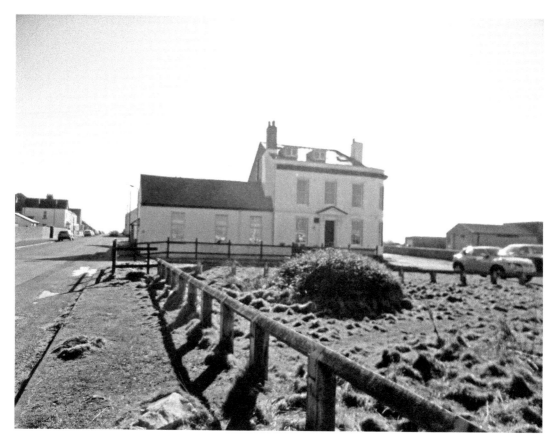

Roa Island Hotel.

The diary is a record of annual tasks undertaken by the farmer, weather, grain yield and prices. His mixed farm was located around where the Town Hall is now and there is a sandstone wall at the corner of Schneider Square and Greengate Street, which is possibly the last surviving remnant of this farm and its buildings. Sometimes he touches on major incidents, which would cause even more change to the town – for example the great storm in 1852. This destroyed the pier at Roa Island and resulted in John Abel Smith selling the island to Furness Railway at a bargain basement price instead of the higher price he had been negotiating. Fisher refers to this event thus: 'a perfect hurricane doing great damage all over the country'.

He appears to take the changes in his stride and his daily life is reported in the same matter of fact way. His farming year is spelt out for us and it provides an insight into the work and regular pattern of tasks that farmers had undertaken for centuries. For example, in 1845, he had 'begun to Shear Septr 13 Shore out White grain very fine weather for 3 week only lost ¼ of a day' (the grammar and spelling is his own). Interspersed with the agricultural timetable we are treated to a range of personal and local social events and occurrences. Sometimes the catalogue of death and disaster is quite overwhelming, but it

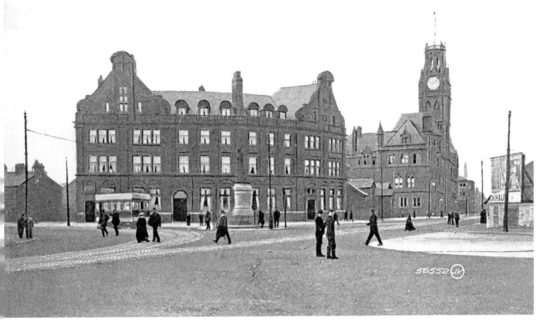

Schneider Square.

gives us an idea of how fragile life could be in the early nineteenth century. In November 1846 there is a veritable catalogue of disaster:

> Died at Ulverston in child-bed aged 33 years Martha the truly amiable and beloved wife of John Denny druggist. Mrs Walker of North Scale Ile of Walney Died advanced years. Wm Danson the last surviving son of Sarah Danson of Dalton died aged 25 years... Richd Robinson Butcher of lane Hous near Ulverstone put an end to his Life by handing (hanging) himself in a corner (coroner) Jurey sat upon the Body Virdict Temperry Insanaty. Died in Octr a child of James Tysons Barrow aged about 11 months.

Fisher remarks upon events that are very relevant in the history of Barrow, but he reports on them in the same measured way that he reports his crop sowing. We read that on 30 April 1846, 'The locomotive engin belonging to the Furness Railway was for the first time driven up to Kirkby Ireleth. After staying for some time she departed for Barrow.'

Again on 10 May he remarks in the same way: 'Henry Houghton a youth 16 years of age unfortunately fell under one of the Waggons of the furness Railway and had his legs so crushed that he died a few days after of inflammation' (infection).

These industrial accidents are reported throughout and are an indication of the lack of awareness of health and safety – these accidents were so common that little remark is made beyond the fact.

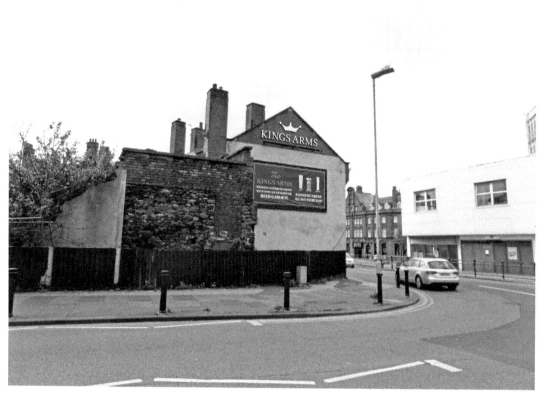

Old Wall, Fisher's Farm.

On a social level the diaries are fascinating, especially for those few who can truly claim to be Barrovians. Some of the names he mentions are still prevalent in Furness and the references are exciting for family historians. We see the family associations, the pastimes and the lighter side of early nineteenth-century life. Visits to church are recorded and of course this would be a meeting place for friends on the one free day of the week. He mentions the launch of the first ship in Barrow in September 1852, the *Jane Roper*: 'the day was beautiful all the Vessels had their Flags hoisted'. This might have been a special day that he actually witnessed. He recounts when the family socialise or have visitors, such Agnes Fisher from Liverpool (a relation) and Agnes Clark from Ulverston, who visited the same day as Thomas Bowes from Fenwick.

All of this detail paints a vivid picture and highlights how ordinary life in the village went on despite the rapid changes happening around them. Presumably the full impact was not realised until after Fisher's death. The diaries are intriguing and tantalising: who would not like to follow up on some of the stories to find out what happened next? Some of the gruesome stories are very graphic, notably the domestic accidents involving open fires and voluminous clothes, which seemed fairly commonplace at this time. The larger industrial tragedies demonstrate how far we have come with safe working practices and health and safety legislation, the hazards now hopefully less than then. It is also worth noting the mention of commonplace tragedies at sea, both with the sinking of ships and boats in bad weather, drownings around the treacherous mud flats of Morecambe Bay and the Duddon Estuary. The lugubrious list of other deaths is staggering: infections, cholera, smallpox, accidental consumption of poison, childbirth, 'inflamation of the windpipe' – probably diphtheria or quinsy – and falls from horses. These horrible items are no more remarked upon than all the rest, which shows that Fisher and his contemporaries probably accepted all this as part of normal life in a way that we would not.

Fisher's own family was not exempt from tragedy and of his six offspring two died in early middle age, both before their father. The others married and dispersed. One son mentioned in the diary left for America in 1844 and only returned in 1856 and then once more in 1869 after both his parents had died. Fisher himself died in 1861 at the remarkably good age of eighty-five. In 1874 their eldest son Richard sold the farm to Barrow-in-Furness Corporation and the buildings was demolished. Eventually no trace of the farm was left and a solitary rough stone wall is allegedly all that is left in testament to its existence.

Acknowledgements

A book like this can't be written without help from certain institutions and publications and I acknowledge them here. Every effort has been made to credit the use of photographs and documents and to obtain permission for copyright material in this book. However if we have inadvertently used copyright material without permission or acknowledgement we apologise and we will make the necessary correction at the first opportunity.

The publisher and author would like to thank the following people for permission to use copyright material in this book: Cumbria Archives and the Barrow Public Library, Sabine Skae from the Dock Museum Barrow, Keith Johnson from the Barrow Borough Council, English Heritage, National Trust, Marion McClintock of Cumberland and Westmorland Antiquarian and Archaeological Society, Jackie Baxter of Abbey Mill, and Nathaniel Jepson and Katy Millard (air-raid shelter pictures) for the use of images and photography. A special mention to Matthew, Jemma, Rafferty and Ronnie Johnston, who gave photos and information of Harper Gaythorpe's house; they are currently renovating this as a family home. I would like to acknowledge the Barrow Civic Society Chairman Vanessa Allen, Lucy Ronald EH, Furness Abbey, for their assistance in acquiring permissions, information and images.

I would like to acknowledge the use of the following publications used in researching this book:

Appley, Stuart, Furness Hidden Heritage Blogspot (and for the personal tour of Abbotswood)
Barnes F., *Barrow and District*
Barrow Borough Council, 'Stories behind the Stones Rod White'
Barrow in Furness Harbour (Oxford Archaeology North, 2003)
Beck, Thomas, *Annales Furnessienses*
Collective works of Alice Leach
Collective works of Bryn Trescathric
Coupe J, Salisbury C., *Mesolithic Occupation of Mill Dam Meadow* (Gleaston, 2004)
'Dalton Archaeological Report: Urban Survey', English Heritage
'Dalton to Roose Greenway: Archaeological Watching Brief' (Oxford Archaeology North, 2009)
History Detectives Project, Bluebirds Study Centre: Early Barrow and Cemetery, (G. Jepson, 2009)
Jepson, Nathaniel, *The Castle that Time Forgot: An Archaeological and Geophysical Report* (2007)
The Diary of William Fisher, Occasional Paper Number 15 (1986)
Walton, James E., *A History of Dalton-in-Furness*
West, Thomas, *Antiquities of Furness*